BEING YOU, BEING HAPPY

How to Love Yourself and Achieve Your Dreams

Livia Severino ♡

BEING YOU, BEING HAPPY

HOW TO LOVE YOURSELF AND ACHIEVE YOUR DREAMS

LIVIA SEVERINO

NEW DEGREE PRESS

COPYRIGHT © 2021 LIVIA SEVERINO

BEING YOU, BEING HAPPY
HOW TO LOVE YOURSELF AND ACHIEVE YOUR DREAMS

ISBN   978-1-63676-799-4 *Paperback*
         978-1-63676-875-5 *Kindle Ebook*
         978-1-63676-876-2 *Ebook*

For my loving and supportive parents, Steph and Vic,

thank you for being the best parents I could have asked for.

TABLE OF CONTENTS

AUTHOR'S NOTE

"Your beliefs become your thoughts, your thoughts become your words, your words become your actions, your actions become your habits, your habits become your values, your values become your destiny."

—MAHATMA GANDHI; ONE OF THE TWENTIETH CENTURY'S
GREATEST POLITICAL AND SPIRITUAL LEADERS

Dear Reader,

Imagine you are seven years old again. You are playing outside with all your friends, not a care in the world. You have things you love to do, like dancing, swimming, and soccer. One day you dream of becoming a vet or a mermaid, whichever is easier.

Now imagine you are twelve years old. You wake up, and the only thing on your mind is your changing body. You start avoiding mirrors and wearing extra baggy clothes to hide your insecurities. You flip through magazines your mom left on the couch, and all you see is one body type represented. You wonder if this is the gold standard and if you're supposed to look like this. At lunch, you start eating less and sometimes "forget to eat." You stop being as carefree as you once were. You change your style, your hair, aspects of your personality just so you can fit in with the "cool" kids.

At seventeen, you struggle to love yourself and continue to feel like you aren't good enough. Social media is now the basis of your social life. Every day you scroll through images of models and celebrities; the constant comparison is exhausting, but you can't stop. You now base your worth on the number of likes your pictures get. It's not about who you are as a person. It's about who you hang out with, what parties you go to, and who likes who.

When you are twenty-one, you don't have any passions. What you once loved as a seven-year-old, you no longer have time for. You feel stuck and not sure what your purpose is. All of your friends have jobs and seem to have it figured out, but you feel lost. If you could have it your way, you would start your own design company. But self-doubt, fear, and worry about what others would think stops you from going after this dream.

The timelines may be different for you, but the message is still the same. At times in our lives, often starting as young as age nine, we begin to feel self-conscious and insecure about our bodies and achievements. We start comparing ourselves to the outside world. We fight out genetics to look a certain way. We chase society's standards in order to "be happy." We forget what matters most in life: who we are and how we love.

Since I was eleven, I have spent so much of my life trying to fight who I am and how I look. I have broken down and cried over the scale. I have tortured my body and my mind to try to look like someone else. I have distanced myself from who I am to live up to a standard I imposed on myself. I have tried to be perfect, tried to fit in, tried to be a size two. For eleven years, I have held myself back from truly living and going after the life I want.

Perhaps you can relate to this. Maybe you have, like me, turned to self-help books and memoirs, looking to grow and feel inspired. I loved the books I read, but I realized a pattern. Someone in their thirties or forties wrote every book I read about their past experiences and recent adult years. Their audiences mostly consisted of men and women in their age group. I got a great deal out of those books, but I wished there was something out there that talked about growing up with the experiences I was and am currently facing: being a young adult, social media, struggling with motivation, and comparison. So instead of continuing to search for that book, I am writing it.

One of my favorite things to do is to sit down with a friend and just talk. We talk about shallow stuff, our love interests, celebrities, or school gossip. But we also have deeper, more vulnerable conversations about our fears and insecurities. We can be completely open about how we are feeling. That means no filters and no "life is great, and everything is perfect." We can be our authentic selves.

The intent of this books is just that: a conversation with a friend. (I also hope it's motivational and gives some great advice, too.)

What would bring me the utmost happiness is for this book to help you navigate a challenge that you are currently facing or may face in the future. I hope that by sharing my experiences and being completely open about what I went through, how I felt, and how I rose above it all, I can provide you with insight into dealing with similar situations.

Social media drives us to compare our lives with others and judge ourselves against altered images, leaving us feeling insecure. I have fallen victim to the social media mind games on more than one occasion. What I have realized in recent years is social media is a highlight reel. Whether you're an ordinary person, a model, or an influencer, we all have insecurities we believe we need to hide. I believe when we talk openly about our insecurities and fears, we regain power and begin to make peace with those insecurities—like I made peace with the dark hair on my arms. After I battled my body for years, I confronted my fear and overcame my eating disorder. Once I finally let go and appreciated what I was given, I learned to love myself as I am. And now, I am happier than I have ever been.

I am not writing this because I believe I have it all figured out or because I think my advice is the best out there. That is not the reason I am writing this at all. I am writing this because I am still learning, still dealing with heartbreak, still struggling with loving myself, still constantly learning about who I am and who I want to be. I am writing this because I, too, will benefit from this.

A lot of what I will write about in these chapters may not pertain to you, but hopefully, you will gain a new understanding out of my stories and my learning experiences... even if it is an example of how *not* to handle a situation—or even if my stories just give you a good laugh.

This book infuses advice from people in my life, advice derived from my own experiences, and advice I have compiled from the books and podcasts I have consumed. This book will focus on our mindsets and how we have the power to change the narrative and live happier despite our circumstances. The purpose of this book is to inspire you to follow your passions, do things for yourself, live life bravely, and love yourself as you are. I will share how I healed my relationship with my body. I will talk openly about my relationships, my fears, my insecurities. I will be vulnerable, I will be open, and I won't hold back.

I no longer want to be the reason why I am unhappy. I choose to be me, and that means creating, finding, and enjoying happiness whenever possible.

Being You, Being Happy is intended to remind you that you are not alone in any of your struggles. We all face hard times, but they challenge us to grow, become grounded, and bring us to where we are supposed to be. We are here to live *our* lives—no one else's. I want you to realize your potential and go after the life you dreamed of. I want you to live life on your terms and not for external validation. I want you to be your happiest version of yourself.

So, let's talk. Let's get real.

PART ONE:

LOOKS

CHAPTER 1

LEAN INTO BODY LOVE

———

"Life is so much more beautiful and complex than a number on a scale."

—*TESS MUNSTER; MODEL*

I love cake. Like, seriously, I *love cake.* I might be totally full from dinner, but as soon as the cake comes out, it is as if I haven't eaten all day. (Carrot cake is my favorite.)

For my eighteenth birthday, I told my mom I didn't want cake. I didn't want a celebration at all, for that matter—no friends, no yummy dinner, and no cake. Presents were the exception. All I wanted was a taco salad for dinner: romaine lettuce, turkey meat, and a dash of salsa on top. I wanted none of the fun stuff. This was in 2016, a year into my eating disorder.

Almost every morning for four months, I woke up and immediately weighed myself—a moment that would determine my whole day. My alarm would ring at 6:30 a.m., the sound of bells reverberating around the room as I forced my body out of the warm cave of my bed. I would throw my covers to the side, slip off the edge, and reluctantly pull myself to the bathroom.

It was another morning, a different day, but somehow the same as the day before.

I'd do it again. I'd take off my oversized pajamas as the cold tile sent chills up my feet, creating a sea of goose bumps across my arms, adrenaline tingling throughout my body. *What would today be? A good day? A bad day? Only one way to find out.* I would wait as the scale reset itself to zero. Slowly, right foot first, left foot second, I would climb onto the silver, electric scale I allowed to determine my worth, mood, who I was as a person, and how much I would punish myself.

The seconds would feel like minutes as the tiny screen lit up to once again tell me my fate. Looking back at me was the number that either said, "You failed," or "You are doing great. Keep it up." If that number was even 0.2 pounds higher than the day before, I would feel like I was spiraling. (It is natural to fluctuate between five and six pounds per day.) I anticipated a downward tumble into more and more weight gain, eventually creeping back to my starting point. I would feel like a failure, so I would do more. I would be stronger. I would resist more. *Again and again.*

From 2015 to 2019, I counted every single calorie that crossed my lips.

I walked to and from school every day in high school, except for the occasional day where my mom drove me because of the snow or frigid temperatures: the expected but always detested New England winter days. On my walks, which were thirty minutes (depending on whether I made every pedestrian light, a little game I would play with myself), I would count. I would count the calories I ate for breakfast and the calories I would eat later as I had already planned out my meals for the day and for the week. I would count the calories, then recount to make sure I wasn't overeating. I would then re-recount because you can never be too sure. On my way home, I would count again.

After school and before hours of studying, I would make a quick pit-stop at home to change before going to the gym. Even though I was tired after a long day of school, my eating disorder (ED) and obsessive need to follow a strict routine took control, forcing me to the gym every day. Another thirty-minute walk later—no pedestrian light—I would be at the gym, ready to count. I would count the calories I burned running on the treadmill, gliding on the elliptical, and in the group fitness class I would attend. Sometimes it would be two classes. I would subtract the calories I ate from the ones I burned, making sure I was on target. At home, I would check the steps on my Fitbit, 20,000, another tick mark. *Hopefully, the scale would reward me for my hard work.*

Some days I would mess up. My body would take over my mind and say: *This girl needs to eat. Make her eat everything in the cabinet.* I would binge, then break down in tears thinking I was "weak," and haul myself to the gym to "work it off." Sometimes, this would mean going back to the gym at 9 p.m., even though my mom would plead for me to stay home.

For over a year, I lived for the sole purpose of shrinking my body. I spent hours each day counting calories and, later, macros as well (the grams of fat, carbs, and protein I ate). I weighed my food to make sure I was on track. I lashed out at my parents for any minor thing, including eating one blueberry I had weighed out. I said no to dinners out with my family and friends because I was afraid of overeating, and because of that, I lost so much quality time that I could have spent with them. I didn't go out to parties because I was too self-conscious about the way I looked, and in turn, I missed out on making so many memories. I made excuses not to hang out with my then-boyfriend—just so I could go to the gym. I said no to cake on my birthday. I said no to enjoying life and being free. I was so obsessed with dieting, with calorie counting, with exercising, with my body, that I lost myself.

And what started it? What triggered this need to limit my happiness for the goal of a slimmer body? Society and the swirling ideas that a woman's worth is carried in the body she lives in, and that a smaller, thinner body is valued more than a bigger frame.

Our society makes it seem as though only one body type is beautiful, while the rest are "acceptable," "average," or "needing improvement." We see this in magazines' images of size two models, praise of celebrities' "abs" or "bikini bodies" on gossip websites, and stick figure mannequins at clothing stores. We see it in the limited range of sizes that most retailers carry and the countless ads for diet programs and detox teas. All-day long, messages surround that either directly or indirectly tell us we need to be skinnier, more toned, and smaller.

I thought my worth was carried in the way I looked—or, more specifically, in what my body looked like. I thought if I could "fix" my body and make it smaller, I would be considered attractive. I would not have any problems. I would be worthy. I would be worthy *because* of my body, not because of who I was as a person, my abilities, kindness, or energy. That is what I took away from the messaging on social media, the commercials on TV, the advertisements in magazines, the way people talked about celebrities. That is what I learned as early as eleven years old: that worth was measured by the size of your jeans and not the size of your heart.

I am naturally curvy. I have muscle. I have fat. I have thighs, a waist, and hips that make it nearly impossible to find jeans that fit perfectly. I do not have society's narrow version of the "ideal body type." But I let this ideal and the view I had of myself take over. I missed out on time with loved ones, laughs, and happiness—just so I would fit into society's narrow range of beauty. I tried to do the impossible: to take my curvy frame and shrink it to nothing—to literally defy nature and take a body that is healthy at 140–150 pounds and shrink it to 125 pounds or lower. I thought by reaching this number, by reaching this gold standard body type, I would be happy. I thought I would feel beautiful and I would have no insecurities. I thought I would feel worthy. Instead, I was miserable.

Over a year into my "weight loss" journey (unknown to my family and friends as an eating disorder), I hit my "goal" weight. One morning after the long seconds passed, I stared down at my feet to the number I had been praying for: 125 pounds. I thought I would feel elated, relieved, that I would be done. I did not feel any of those things. Instead, the voice inside me whispered: *Cool, you're not done yet.*

The least I ever weighed was 123 pounds. To some, this may be a high weight. To others, this may be a natural set point, and to some, this might not be possible. For me, this was not where my body wanted to be. My body cried for help as it tried to talk to me in every conceivable way. My body sent me signals by making my hair fall out, making me cold even when it was in the middle of summer, making my face look ill, and making me depressed. In December 2016, I hit a new low when I hung over the toilet seat, willing myself to get rid of the binge I just consumed. I couldn't do it. I lay on the cold tile of the bathroom where my mood was determined every morning, and I cried, finally admitting to myself for the first time in fifteen months: *I had a problem.*

MY TURNING POINT

It did not happen overnight. But after admitting I had a problem, I knew I needed to make a change in how I viewed food. So, I decided to turn my attention to learning more about nutrition. I read book after book. I learned how to take care of my body in a *healthy* way. I learned to view food as fuel, as energy. I learned eating too little can cause your body to shut down and hold on to anything it can because it is trying to keep you alive. *No wonder it took so long to get to my "goal" weight: my body was fighting to protect me.* I stopped viewing food just as calories to avoid and started viewing it as essential vitamins, minerals, and other compounds that make up my cells, that can act as medicine and cure me from the inside out. For the first time in months, I saw food as a friend, not as an enemy.

However, my original monster, restriction, morphed into an entirely new beast: an obsession with health. I hid my persistent body dysmorphia and subsequent new eating disorder: orthorexia (an unhealthy obsession with healthy food), under the guise of a new passion for nutrition.

Although my image around exercise and my body had changed since my lowest point, my mind had not yet healed. I continued to be ruled by food, but this time by nutritional benefits rather than calories. Anything not deemed "healthy," I avoided—including my beloved cake.

I continued to count calories, allowing myself more than before, but still monitoring my daily intake. I took up different patterns of eating: paleo, vegan, vegetarian, pescatarian— anything that restricted a category of less nutritious foods. I navigated my first year of college as a vegan for the sole reason of avoiding the dreaded "freshman fifteen" (which I ended up gaining, and not in an enjoyable way).

While I was no longer starving my body and punishing it for wanting to keep me alive. I was still not allowing my body to decide what it needed. I was still hyper-focused on the way I looked. I was still anxious about eating. I said no to foods I enjoyed and tried to convince myself that roasted Japanese sweet potatoes taste like candy. (I can confidently tell you now they do not taste like candy, but they are delicious.) I was eating enough, eating healthily, but my obsession with controlling what I ate, when I ate, and how much I ate was unhealthy.

In 2016, I was a teenager in high school who felt insecure about her body. As a size eight, I felt bigger than all my friends and wanted to feel prettier. I listened to messaging on social media and forced my body to become smaller. The media convinced me being thin was the magical panacea for all my problems. But even after losing thirty to forty pounds, I did not gain confidence. I didn't lose all my insecurities. I didn't become popular and get the life I dreamed of. Instead, I gained an unhealthy relationship with food and with my body that, even five years later, I still struggle with.

It was not until the spring of my junior year of college, when I went abroad to London that I finally decided once and for all to break free of the chains. After five years of calorie counting, diets, and diet culture dictating what I should and shouldn't eat, I was finally going to trust myself and allow my body to tell me what it needed. I vowed to myself to no longer chase society's beauty ideal; instead, the only thing I would chase would be my happiness. I had stopped being happy to pursue the "perfect body." I finally realized that the perfect body does not exist. We are never 100 percent pleased with what we have. I know this because even at my lowest weight, where I thought I would be happy, I clearly wasn't.

I told my body in 2016 that I didn't trust it and I didn't like it. I punished it for over a year to look like something that was not attainable for me. My body and I were at war with each other. Each year since I decided to heal, we have made amends, and my thoughts surrounding my body image have become lighter. Each year I have learned to love myself a little more. It has not been a short road. But the day I stopped lying to myself, stopped telling myself I was fine and I was "healthy," was the day I started to heal.

I healed my relationship with my body and food slowly. It started with some major changes, such as breaking up with the scale (both the food scale and the one that lived on my bathroom floor). To this day, I don't know what I weigh unless I go to the doctor's office, and even then, I try not to look. This is what works for me and my mental health. Now, I like to depend on how I feel rather than how I should feel based on a number. I also *finally* deleted my calorie counting apps and told my parents. Having someone support you in recovery is not only extremely helpful; it is necessary. They didn't judge, and they didn't question. Instead, they were there for me in any way that I needed. I was recovering for myself and for them. I no longer wanted them to be worried. I wanted to be their daughter again—not the moody, obsessed woman I had become.

I wanted to be me again.

Today, I am in a happy medium. Most days, I love my body and embrace my curves. But some days, I struggle with body love and acceptance. Some days I call my mom crying over my curves. Nothing in life is black and white. One day I will be dancing around my bedroom in my underwear because of how grateful I am to be me. The next day, I might avoid looking in the mirror. And that is okay. On the days when it is harder to love or accept my body as it is, I allow myself to have those feelings but then give myself love in other areas. *Feeling a little puffy and swollen today? That's all right. Your butt looks great, by the way.*

The biggest difference is that I no longer punish myself. I no longer workout to burn calories. I no longer obsessively control what I eat. Instead, I work out as a celebration of what I can do. I move my body in a way that feels good. I do it for the endorphins, to improve my mental health, and to become stronger. Today, I eat to heal my body. I eat foods that taste good. I eat salads, and I eat pizza. Some days I will have an apple for dessert, and other days I'll get ice cream with friends. My body tells me what to eat—not my brain, not diet culture, not an app.

Today, I am happier than I have ever been because I have learned to accept myself as I am, to love my body as it is and as it wants to be. This didn't happen all of a sudden. It took me years to get to where I am now. But the moment I was honest with myself and admitted I wasn't truly happy, I knew I had a problem. That was when the healing began. That was when I sought help. When I told my parents. When I went to therapy. When I removed triggers, unfollowed accounts, deleted apps, that was when I started looking in the mirror and seeing more than just a body.

A SAD REALITY

Unfortunately, my story is not rare. Ninety-five percent of individuals who have eating disorders are between the ages of twelve and twenty-five, with children as young as six wanting to be thinner ("Body Image & Eating Disorders," 2018). The US Department of Health and Human Services reported that "almost half of American children between first and third grade want to be thinner and half of nine and ten-year-old girls are dieting." These statistics are sad but not surprising. Thanks to the diet industry, social media, and marketing, boys and girls are told from a young age that certain body types are "healthy" and "good," and so, by default, others aren't. Fortunately, messaging has changed over the years with the body positivity movement. Many brands are moving away from traditional models to models of varying sizes, shapes, and skin colors. This is a huge improvement, but nevertheless, eating disorders, poor self-esteem, and body image issues are increasingly prevalent.

Studies show approximately 50 percent of girls and 30 percent of boys dislike their bodies between the ages of ten and thirteen, and 60 percent of adult women and 40 percent of adult men have a negative body image (Muhlheim, 2021).

Body image issues are not tied to a specific gender or specific individuals. Rather, they are societal problems stemming from dangerous messaging.

YOUR WORTH IS NOT DETERMINED BY YOUR WEIGHT

There is so much more to life than constant dieting, hating your body and trying to change it, and being hungry all the time because you are not happy with what you currently have. Losing weight is not your life's purpose. You were not put on this planet to diet your life away or to be unhappy until you achieve a certain image in your head. In the past, I put my life and happiness on pause to shrink my body. I thought that having a thin body would make me happier, more attractive, and more valuable. I believed that the smaller my body became, the happier I would become. But instead of being happier, I became more unhappy and detached. Each pound I lost took me further away from who I was. I was not just shrinking my body. I was eliminating the people I loved. I was taking joy away from my experiences. I was torturing my mental state. All I could talk about and think about was food. I had no room to be happy because my energy was focused elsewhere. My mindset kept me from experiencing life to its fullest.

The way you look is the least interesting thing about you. What matters is who you are, how you make people feel, and the way you live your life. Although I have my ups and downs to this day with my body (and we all do), I have been able to make peace with my curves. I have freed up so much time by not obsessing. I have laughed more, smiled more, enjoyed life more, and become closer to the woman I want to be. I was the one who tried to shrink my body, but I was also the one who learned to listen to my body again, to love my insecurities and my curvy figure, to be okay with fluctuations, and to embrace my genetics.

It may take time. It may take years. It may take struggles similar or dissimilar to mine. However long it takes, however it has to happen, I hope that one day you are able to love yourself exactly as you are. It is the best gift you can ever give yourself, and it is entirely up to you and entirely achievable.

Even though it took me five years, today, I make the best carrot cake. And make it whenever I want. I enjoy a big slab of cake with zero guilt and all joy. I'll even have seconds.

WHAT HAS HELPED ME HEAL MY RELATIONSHIP WITH MY BODY:

Notice your triggers

- A trigger is a stimulus that activates a response in the body, usually a negative response. Triggers come in all shapes and forms and can be social, situational, environmental, psychological, or physiological. An example of a trigger for me when I was in my orthorexia stage was nutrition labels. Whenever I saw a food with a nutrition label, I had to read it, and certain criteria had to be met before I ate it. A lot of times, even if I was hungry, I would not eat it because I wouldn't deem the food "healthy" enough.

- Becoming aware of and identifying your triggers is a huge step in healing your relationship with your body. But this is also hard, and it takes a lot of self-awareness and honesty. Some of you may already know your triggers, and that is great! But some triggers may not be easily identifiable. The best way I have found in finding the source is to write down a chain of events, including everyone and everything involved, and mentally play detective to find a potential triggering factor.

- Once you recognize your triggers, you can start the healing by distancing yourself from the source, cutting it out entirely, disrupting the connection, or changing and adjusting how you view it. For instance, if your trigger is a certain celebrity, you can unfollow their accounts. If your trigger is seeing a certain food that causes you to binge, stop buying the food or have someone hide it. When you see the food and feel a need to binge, distance yourself and go engage in another activity. Maybe your Fitbit is a trigger that causes obsessive thoughts. Try ditching the watch for a week or two and see how you feel. There are many ways to go about removing triggers: this stage is highly personal so find what works for you.

Break up with the apps, scale, diet blogs, restrictive diet accounts

- This is one of the biggest things that helped me when I was healing my relationship with my body and food. When I was deep into my eating disorder, I followed hundreds of workout accounts, macro-counting accounts, and "inspiration" accounts of women with my ideal body type. Seeing these images all day, every day, caused me to be constantly thinking of food and my body. Even though I thought I was using these accounts as inspiration, all they did was make me feel worse and restrict myself more. There is nothing wrong with the content they were posting. But personally, it was not healthy for me to be consuming it. A digital detox improved my mental health tremendously, especially when I swapped out the diet culture accounts and instead followed body positive, body neutral, and recovery accounts.

Get in touch with your body

- Get to know your body. You live in your body your whole life, and many of us don't ever spend the time to really get to know it. Get to know the foods that your body reacts to negatively and the foods that energize your body. Do different types of workouts to learn which ones your body likes and which ones cause too much fatigue. Without judgment, get in front of the mirror and take the time to really look at your body. Look at your curves, your markings, your freckles, scars, moles. Dedicate however long you need to get in touch with your body and its workings. Your body is your forever home. It is worth getting to know.

Move your body in ways that feel good and are empowering

- I started working out to lose weight. I viewed exercise as punishment, or a means to be able to eat more. In my mind, going to the gym was "work." One day, after I was in my healing process, I woke up not in the mood to workout. It was a day I usually worked out, and I already had a workout planned, my alarm set to wake me up early, and my workout clothes laid out. That was the first time I woke up, decided, "Nah, I'm not in the mood," and went back to bed. And guess what happened? I didn't die. I didn't gain three pounds in a day. I didn't experience any repercussions I feared would happen if I skipped a workout. Yes, working out is good and necessary for mental and physical health. But that day I finally had the epiphany that exercise is supposed to be enjoyable. That day of finally listening to my body's wants and needs showed me as long as I move my body in ways that feel good to me, it does not matter what workout I do. The more I moved my body, not as punishment, but in an enjoyable way, the better I took care of my body, and the more connected I felt to it.

Practice body neutrality

- Body neutrality is all about accepting your body as it is and focusing more on how you feel rather than on how you look. Body neutrality emphasizes it is okay not to love your body every day or at all, but what's most important is listening to your body's needs and catering to those. Body neutrality is about seeing your body beyond its physical appearance and instead valuing and appreciating its abilities and what it does for you.

- Ways to practice body neutrality:

  - Eat intuitively. Eat food you want to eat, food that nourishes you and tastes good to you. Sometimes your body wants a salad, other times it wants potato chips.

  - Do not judge, criticize, or shame your body or anyone else's. Everyone has different genetics.

  - Exercise to move your body and feel good. Partake in exercises you enjoy.

Seek counseling or support from a loved one

- Therapy and confiding in a loved one were game changers. Talking to someone I felt safe with challenged me to dig deep and identify my internal wounds and areas in my life that needed healing. It was through talking in therapy I realized why I so desperately needed to calorie count and control my eating and exercise. It was in therapy I confessed I felt like a failure if I didn't track perfectly or if I gained weight. It was through a conversation with my mom before leaving for study abroad when I admitted to her and myself I was still in a negative space with my body and food. All of those conversations were hard to have, but as soon as I said my thoughts out loud and to someone, it brought me out of my head and swirling negative talk into seeing myself and what I was doing from an outside perspective. The conversations made me want to make a change because I now had someone who knew what I was thinking. Someone who was in my corner rooting for me to work on myself. It set me on a path to make a change and heal what was not working.

Make a list

- Now, this may be the Virgo in me, but I love a good list. I find making lists to be therapeutic because it forces me to stop and think. And when you write things down, they feel more concrete. So, I encourage you to make some lists: lists of things you are grateful for, things you love about your body, some talents you have. Any positive, energizing, and uplifting list! Get out of your head and go-go-go life for a second and take a moment to appreciate your abilities, blessings, body, family, experiences. So much of our lives are spent picking apart our bodies and flaws. Take the time now to write what you love about your body, how it works, and what it does.

- The next time you are not feeling great and start nit-picking your body, stop, and give it a compliment from your list instead.

CHAPTER 2

INSECURITIES AND VULNERABILITIES

"You have been criticizing yourself for years, and it hasn't worked. Try approving of yourself and see what happens."

—LOUISE HAY; AUTHOR

I started puberty in the fifth grade, long before any of my friends. That is when my insecurities first started bubbling up. I was the only fifth grader—or, for that matter, middle schooler—with boobs and acne. One day I was a happy flat chested ten-year-old, and the next, I was shopping for bras and tampons at Target with my mom. The saving grace of it all was the fun-colored bras I got to wear.

As my body changed, I became increasingly uncomfortable in my own skin. My boobs were growing, my hair was growing in places I didn't know were possible, little red bumps started making unwelcome appearances, and everything just kept getting bigger! I didn't know what to do or how to handle it, but luckily I had the perfect trick. And that trick was a pink sweatshirt with "Aeropostale" written in big swirling white cursive letters across my chest. I wore that sweatshirt every day of fifth grade. That sweatshirt was my armor. That sweatshirt allowed me to hide my maturing body from the world. It allowed me to still fit in with my friends whose bodies weren't changing like mine was.

One day in the sixth grade, in Spanish class to be exact, I was sitting next to my two guy friends as we worked on a group project together. We were busy drawing a cityscape and writing what each thing was in Spanish. I still remember the word *calle* (street) because of that project. I raised my arm slightly after the whole sweatshirt phase, and my guy friend sitting next to me gasped in horror.

"Ew, did you forget to shave? You look like a boy!" He teased in response to my armpit hair. I had not shaved in a few days, and I am Italian with dark hair and pale skin, so you get the gist. My other friend snorted with laughter at his comment. I put my hand down immediately, the blood rushing to my cheeks. I sat there silently while they continued to draw. Their laughter still replayed in my mind as I fought tears that began to flood my eyes. All I wanted to do was hide under my desk. *I wish I still had that pink sweatshirt to hide behind*, I thought.

In seventh grade, that same boy made a comment about how I had hairier arms than my seventh grade "boyfriend." Our arms were resting on the table as my whole friend group gathered in our lunch pod, eating and enjoying our favorite time of the school day. As we all talked and laughed, that boy yet again pointed out my dark thick hair remarking, "Wow, Livia, your arms are hairier than Nic's." I was mortified. Everyone heard and started laughing *and* agreeing. I had never noticed. I never even thought twice about my arm hair, nor did I think anyone else did.

Since that moment, I have battled internally with my arm hair, thinking and researching endless ways to "fix" the problem. Ultimately, I decided not to do anything because shaving my arms or bleaching them would just mean years of doing just that (and hours taken from my life to upkeep it all). Instead, I decided to change my perspective.

I worked to reframe how I viewed my insecurities, changing it from being something that made me "unattractive" to insecurities being something everyone deals with, and no one notices a much as I do. I spent time appreciating all that I do have and love. I love the thick dark curly hair on my head, which comes from my Italian heritage. My arm hair is just a tradeoff and a marking of where I come from. I readjusted my outlook; time, money, and energy are valuable, and I have a choice of how to spend them. I could spend them changing my looks or spend them on quality time with loved ones, doing things I enjoy, and bettering myself. For me, that choice was easy.

I did not want to spend the time and effort changing what I was insecure about, nor did I want them to hold me back, so I decided going forward, I would embrace my hairy arms and move on with my life. How freeing!

Over the years, I have struggled with many—and I mean *many*—insecurities. Some have carried with me throughout the years, while some come and go.

Let's just get out a list of my insecurities, shall we:

- My hairline

- Cellulite

- Keratosis Pilaris bumps on my arms

- Large arms, broad shoulders, broad rib cage

- My dark body hair all over my body—like seriously can it chill?

- Acne that flares up at the most inopportune time

- My larger thighs and calves

- My moles (there are a lot of them)

- Uneven skin tone

- Dark eye bags and circles

- My bigger, curvier frame

- … And many more

Do any of my insecurities or "imperfections" make me any less interesting, intelligent, beautiful? Nope. Do people look at me and think, *Wow, that girl's hairline is kinda messed up. She probably isn't a good person*? Nope. Even though I know this, my insecurities still get the best of me sometimes. Some days I love my big thighs. I dance in front of the mirror and appreciate all that I was born with. Some days I sit in my room and cry. Some days I think about shaving my arms. Some days I just think, *yeah, they are hairy but also, who cares? It doesn't make me any less of a woman or any less beautiful.* Every day is different. It just depends on what side of the bed you wake up that morning.

Throughout our lives, we encounter certain attributes that we do not love about ourselves. Insecurities are a shared human trait—we all deal with them. The difference between people is how they choose to let their insecurities define them or their experiences. When we are faced with these insecurities, we are given two options: make a change or make amends.

Option 1: Make an effort to change it. Disclaimer: sometimes, things cannot change.

With this option, there often come time and financial components. Did I really want to spend every shower shaving my arms and then feel insecure when they quickly turned stubbly between shavings? Did I want to invest money shaving them, getting them waxed, or getting laser hair removal? Not really.

But it is up to you.

I will say a lot of the time, even if you change *x* (lose weight, get rid of the excess hairs, fix the things you don't like), you will still find ways to be unhappy. We all do. You can make a change, but know that chances are, if you don't figure out what the root of the insecurity is—the thing that is *really* stealing your inner peace—even after the change, you may still feel insecure.

Then there is Option 2: Accept who you are. Accept that we all have our insecurities. Some are easy to overcome, while others may not be easy. Acceptance can be hard because it requires us to give up this frequently false idea that if we push and punish ourselves enough, we will change and be happy. But more often than not, rejecting what we don't like and punishing ourselves brings us further away from where we want to be and into a more negative headspace. It has for me, at least.

Accept your genetics, circumstances, and reality. Accept that insecurities, struggles, and challenges will always arise and be a part of your life, just like they are for everyone else. Accept that, in most cases, it is so much easier to learn to love or accept something than to work to change it or spend time hating it. It is also a much more pleasant way to live if you ask me.

I spent most of my life doing Option 1, but recently I have done the latter: accepting myself as I am. By going with Option 2, I have been so much happier and more confident. Added bonus: more time to spend on other things and less wasted money.

TAKE BACK THE POWER

In all honesty, from what I have learned from my own journey with insecurities is that it is not our insecurities that are the problem. It is our view of them. We give our insecurities power by hiding them away and letting them take control of how we view ourselves. We allow our insecurities to hold us back from wearing certain outfits, from putting on a bathing suit and going in the pool, from relaxing and enjoying the moment because we are too focused on ourselves and how we look. When we talk about our insecurities, we give them less power. The moment I started talking about my cellulite or my hairline to my friends and family, I took power back. And I also got a lot of "Who cares?" or "I didn't even notice!"

By talking about our insecurities, we 1) learn that everyone has them (and a lot of times people are insecure about things you find beautiful); and 2) no one cares about your insecurity. No one is looking at you like you look at you. No one cares if you have cellulite or a few pimples or thin hair. Everyone is so dang self-focused; they don't even notice. And the people who do notice only do so because they are insecure within themselves. It says nothing about you and everything about them.

That boy who pointed out my arm hair was insecure, so he found a way to make himself feel better by bringing someone else down. Since then, no one has said one thing about my arm hair, nor has it held me back in any way unless I have let it. Tearing others down is not a way to cope with your internal feelings. If that boy knew those two comments he made as "jokes" lead to years of insecurity for me, I hope he would have thought twice before saying them or anything similar to anyone else. Think before you speak, even with what you say to yourself.

EVERYONE IS INSECURE IN SOME WAY

Society adds to the insecurity epidemic in more ways than one. For one, most of us have social media flooded with images of gorgeous people who don't have a hair out of place. It is so easy to feel "less than" when this is the content we see day-in and day-out. But even the models and celebrities you see have insecurities. In fact, approximately 40 percent of models have eating disorders, and 62 percent feel pressure to lose weight (Nordqvist, 2007) (Yotka, 2017). These women are forced and prodded to look a certain way, and photographers still go in and edit the pictures, removing any wrinkle, dimple, or fat bulge in sight. The image we see is nothing like the real thing, and yet, we believe that is how we should look. It is no wonder that 69–84 percent of women in the United States are dissatisfied with their bodies (Runfola et al., 2013).

Another reason: sizing. In my wardrobe I have pairs of jeans that are a size six, size eight, size ten, and size twelve. You want to know a secret, *they all fit*! Your size differs between stores and says absolutely nothing about who you are or how healthy you are. I was once a size four, and I was miserable and also extremely unhealthy. I am now a size ten (in most stores), and I am healthy. I eat a balanced diet. I work out every day, I am a spin instructor, and I have run a half marathon. I am three sizes larger and thirty pounds heavier, and I am healthier and so much happier! Our bodies change, our hips get bigger, things expand, things sag and droop down. We can't control the natural aging process—we all go through it. But at the end of the day, we can look at ourselves and say, "Hey, you are beautiful, and your body is strong." Feed yourself with the positive affirmation and love that you give others. You deserve to give yourself the gift of self-love.

It takes time, trust me. I still battle my insecurities constantly. It is not a small feat nor an overnight win. It can be a long and hard journey. But for me, learning to accept my insecurities has been one of the most freeing things I have done, and it can be for you too. I have found that the best place to start is learning to accept yourself as you are.

Here are some things that helped me:

- Allowing yourself to be human, to make mistakes, and to not be perfect.

- Realizing that everyone—and I mean everyone (including Beyoncé)—has insecurities and internal battles.

- Learning to embrace your insecurities and viewing them as markings that contribute to making you more unique, more special, more you; acne, cellulite, moles, scars, stretch marks, hair... whatever they may be.

- Understanding your body is a teammate, a companion, rather than an enemy.

- Reframing the narrative in your head and how you speak to yourself.

Reframing how I viewed my body was what helped me the most. Instead of saying, "My thighs are so big," I think, "Wow, my legs allow me to move and do all these amazing things. They allow me to go all these places and see so many things." Instead of hating my dark body hair, I see it as a token of my heritage and a trade-off to my thick dark eyebrows and hair that I love. I see my markings as reflections of my history. They mark the places I have been: I have my freckles and moles from vacations in the sun. They mark the memories I have made: the burn on my left leg is from when I was carrying a hot pot to a family dinner in Maine and accidentally spilled it. They mark all the wonderful and fun things I have done. I see my body as a reflection of my lineage. I got my dark thick hair from my Italian side, my pear shape and big thighs from my mom's side, and my fair skin from my paternal grandmother. I view my body as mine, and I do things for myself, not for anyone else. My body may not be a size four, it may not have a thigh gap, it may not be tan, cellulite-free, or mole-free—but it is beautiful just the way it is.

Think about all the incredible things your body does: how capable it is, how it keeps you alive, how it protects you when it senses danger, and how it heals you when you are hurt. Your body is on your side. Treat her with respect, treat yourself with compassion, treat yourself with love.

There is a metaphor from Katy Bellotte, a YouTuber and podcaster, who I love. The metaphor is of a cake (*obviously*). Katy says, "Picture a beautiful cake with white frosting and delicate pink flowers. Not all beautiful ingredients went into making that cake; some ingredients are bitter, some are salty, some taste good, and others don't. But all these ingredients together make something that is sweet. That cake, that sweetness, that is joy."

Although we may not love everything about the way we are or the way we look, all of these things make us who we are, and who we are brings joy to those around us. We are supposed to have parts about us that are "bitter" or "salty" because they make us human and tell a story of our past or ancestry.

You are going to have insecurities—you would be a rare breed without them. You can make amends or make changes, you can get comfortable with them, or you can give them power. Whatever you choose to do, I hope you are able to set yourself free. I hope you are able to realize that you are just you—not a perfect human, not existing solely for your looks, but for the impact you make on those around you. I hope you can learn to embrace who you are, the good and the bad. I hope you can take the pressure off and realize that all you ever have to be in this world is yourself, as you are in this moment. The right friends, the right partner, the right people in your life will love you for who you are, imperfections included. Imperfections as a bonus. All the world asks of you is to be yourself and come as you are.

MY TASKS FOR YOU:

Make a list of all of your insecurities, and next to them, write where they all come from

- Can you release some of the pain behind them? Maybe change the narrative and write why you are grateful for that marking?
  - Example: I am insecure about the scar on my right thigh. But it comes from a mole removal that was necessary because the mole looked cancerous. I am grateful for that scar because it removed a potential health issue.

Talk about your insecurities with a trustworthy individual

- Whenever I have talked openly about my insecurities, I have felt lighter about them, felt closer to the person I was sharing them with, and realized my insecurities are not as big of a deal as I think they are.

Practice self-care

- Instead of criticizing what you don't like in the mirror, why not take care of yourself? Self-care comes in many forms: it is not just a spa night at home. Self-care can be cooking your favorite meal, going to a workout class, reading a book, taking a bath, anything you enjoy doing for yourself. Self-care is never selfish. If anything, it is giving yourself more energy so that you have more energy to give to others. I personally think everyone should do at least one form of self-care every day. But if you can't, in times that you feel insecure, anxious, or depleted, I encourage you to take a moment for self-care.

CHAPTER 3

FACETUNE, FOMO, AND THE COMPARISON TRAP

———

"The reason we struggle with insecurity is because we compare our behind-the-scenes with everyone else's highlight reel."

—STEVE FURTICK; PASTOR

When I was thirteen, I desperately wanted a Facebook account, but my mom wouldn't let me get one. This was back in 2011 when social media was still a semi-new idea, and my mom thought I would start chatting with creepy men. Don't worry, Mom, I never did. But what I did do was create a fake account, so I could stay up late messaging my crushes and commenting, "Oh my gosh, you're so pretty" on my friends' pictures. At first, Facebook was a way for me to connect with my friends outside of school hours, ask the boys who they liked (hoping it would be me), and exchange answers to our Spanish homework.

But before long, I had a real Facebook account, as well as an Instagram and a Snapchat. And the platforms were no longer just for gossip and sharing homework answers. Instead, social media became a platform to broadcast your best and most polished self—a platform to show everyone how great your life is, how many parties you attend, how many friends you have. Instead of a way to communicate with childhood friends, social media gained the power to affect an individual's self-esteem and self-worth.

There have always been those triggers that can suddenly take your confidence and shove it down a hill. It may be when you are at the gym and see women with "perfect" bodies running in their tight-fitting expensive matching workout set with their shiny hair swinging back and forth. It could be someone in your life who always looks runway ready as they strut down the sidewalk, surrounded by friends, seemingly living a perfect life. Or it could even be a past self, a picture from prom when your dress hugged you in all the right places, and the flashbacks are memories of pure happiness. A time, and an old body, that you once didn't appreciate but now wish you had again. But now, with the twenty-four seven access to social media, this comparison trap, and subsequent confidence dive is a result of the perfectly edited images we spend hours scrolling through on our feeds.

I, for one, have fallen into the social media comparison trap far too many times. I wake up feeling great, and then an hour after mindlessly scrolling social media, I look at myself in a critical light. I am finding all the ways and areas I need to fix in my life, going from confidence and contentment to insecurity and anxiety with each scroll.

I recently watched an influencer's Instagram story where she talked about her eye bags and the filler she got for them. The next thing I know, I am typing into Google "how much does eye filler cost," and I proceed to spend the next twenty minutes researching and deciding I now need eye filler.

I used to look in the mirror and see my dark eyes, dark brows, pale skin, moles, full lips—now all I see are eye bags in desperate need of filler.

And it's not just the eye bags. It is the cellulite, the stomach pouch, the textured skin that needs fixing. It is the need for a perky round butt, clear glowing skin, voluminous hair, a trimmed jawline, and expertly planned outfits.

It is the need to look a certain way and live a certain lifestyle because of what we see day-in and day-out on our screens.

In a survey of one thousand men and women focused on confidence, body image, and the media, 88 percent of women and 65 percent of men reported they compared their bodies to images they saw on social and traditional media, with half of the men and women saying this comparison was unfavorable and resulted in negative views of self (Murray, 2018).

THE COMPARISON TRAP

In just a few scrolls, I can quickly fall into the trap of comparing my raw life to manipulated and manicured images that make me believe they represent reality. Social media doesn't show the tears, the fights, the hormonal challenges, the bloating. And yet, because I am at a time in my life when I naturally wrestle with body image and self-love, I believe these images reveal the whole story—even when my own social media account portrays images that falsely represent my lived experience. Each time I post a photo, I pick the best one out of hundreds to find the one where I look the best, posed in a way that is most flattering based on years of practice. A photo that captures a second of that day and doesn't show the tears, fights, stress, ups and downs. And yet, time and time again, I compare my life to images I see on social media—when my own images are inaccurate depictions of reality!

Many of us fall into the social media comparison trap, causing us to feel like we need to look like the images we see from the moment we wake up. We strive to achieve a standard that is unattainable. We compare our lives to someone on the internet which we have never met before: we don't know their life story, their insecurities, their highs and lows. And yet we think, "I wish I was like them." Social media can make the most confident of people insecure. As Theodore Roosevelt said over a hundred years ago, "Comparison is the thief of joy," a sentiment no less true today.

We aren't all meant to look alike or achieve the same goals and dreams. Our lives are supposed to be different. There are many people in your social circle who look different from each other and might be accomplishing different things. But you likely have never found yourself picking apart their differences and judging them for what they look like and what their priorities are. Similarly, you don't have to judge yourself. Beauty lies in uniqueness. Why compare yourself to someone else who may be further along in their journey or doing something completely different. That leads to wasted mind space that could be spent going after what you want or experiencing joy.

Countless studies have examined the link between social media use and its negative impacts on mental health. A study by Tiggemann and Slater in 2013 found higher usage of social media correlates with body image issues. I could tell you that from my own experience! Another study at the University of

Pennsylvania investigated the link between social media and well-being. One hundred forty-three undergraduates participated and were randomly assigned to limit a social media platform (Facebook, Snapchat, Instagram) to ten minutes, per platform, per day (Hunt et al., 2018). After a three-week intervention period, participants in the experimental group reported decreases in loneliness and depressive symptoms. And subjects in both the experiment and control groups showed a significant decline in both fear of missing out and anxiety, indicating individuals benefit from self-monitoring their social media use. One of the participants in the study reported that "Not comparing my life to the lives of others had a much stronger impact than I expected, and I felt a lot more positive about myself during those weeks."

You can experiment with yourself. As you scroll, start monitoring whether or not your self-esteem is higher when you use social media less. I know that for me, I can more often than not attribute my bad mood or negative self-talk to the amount of time I spend on screens.

Comparison has been around long before social media was invented. Social comparison theory was developed in 1954 by the social psychologist Leon Festinger. The theory is based on the idea that individuals measure their own personal and social worth compared to how others are doing. Individuals use others as a benchmark to rate themselves. Friends, Instagram models, and celebrity role models become yardsticks for their subjective rating of their own attractiveness and achievements. Festinger found that we compare ourselves in one of two ways: upward comparison (comparing ourselves to people we believe are doing better) and downward comparison (comparing ourselves to people we believe are doing worse). Both cases can have positive or negative implications. We may feel inspired to improve ourselves as a result of the comparison, or we can end up harming our self-esteem and undervaluing who we are. Although upward comparison can be used as "motivation," it can lead to negative habits and feelings of inadequacy. Comparison often leaves us feeling as though we will never be good enough.

At the end of the day, your journey is unique and not a competition. What you want in life, how you experience the world, and the things you value may be vastly different from what someone else wants, needs, and values. The only comparison that matters is the difference between the person you were yesterday to the one you are today. You only ever need to compare yourself with your best performance. Comparison is a negative slippery slope that just holds you back. Everyone is at different places in their lives. Everyone started with different privileges, experiences, and connections. There will always be someone doing better than you in all aspects of life. But what you have that no one else has is that you are the best at being you. No one can take that away. And when you refuse to play the comparison game, comparison can no longer steal your joy.

HOW TO BREAK FREE OF THE COMPARISON TRAP:

1. Spend less time on social media

The more time you spend on social media, the more time you are giving yourself to fall deeper into the comparison trap and feel worse. I have set limits on my social media apps through the settings on my phone, and it has been a game changer! Some of my friends have even deleted their apps off their phones or gone cold-turkey and deleted their accounts completely. Do what works for you. But try challenging yourself with some social media detoxes. You will come to realize how much free time you have when you stop endlessly scrolling through your phone and how much better you might start feeling about yourself. Who knows, maybe you will even discover a new hobby with the time you now have!

To start: Try setting a limit on each app and stick to it. Set a limit that challenges you but also eases you into the detox. For me, I looked at how much time I was spending on each app and then set a timer for half that time.

2. Monitor whom you choose to follow

I used to follow a ton of social media influencers and models, telling myself they were "inspiration." But all that following these accounts did was push me further down the confidence hill (not their fault, but mine). Images of these beautiful women with bodies that I could never achieve left me feeling horrible. These images fueled my addiction to shrinking my body and fighting my genetics. I eventually had enough and unfollowed every account (even some accounts of my friends) that made me feel bad about myself. I started filling my feed with inspirational posts, body-positive accounts, eating disorder recovery accounts, and any account that made me feel empowered. Unfollowing the negative accounts and following positive accounts instead did wonders for my mental health.

In the next few weeks, set some time aside to go through the people you follow and unfollow or mute anyone who leaves you feeling poorly about yourself. Be honest about which accounts are affecting your self-esteem. It may not always be glaringly obvious, but if you spend time looking and zooming in on a picture and then later looking at yourself more critically, it might be an indication you need to get some space from that content.

Next, start following some accounts with positive messaging. Meditation accounts, body-neutrality/positivity accounts, nature photography accounts, you name it! The positive accounts I followed helped me see my body in a better light, and all it took was a few minutes of my day tapping the "unfollow" or the "follow button."

The content we consume can change our energy, our feelings, our internal dialogue, our mood. Continue to be cautious of what you feed yourself.

3. Redirect your focus

Focus on the things that really matter. Social media can be constructive when it is used for sharing valuable information and spreading awareness. However, most of the time (and especially for me), social media is a big ol' unproductive time suck and an addiction. I wake up and often go straight to Instagram. I spend the last hour or more of my day immersed in social media. I browse through social media while in class, while on the toilet, and any time I am bored or procrastinating (including multiple times while writing this book). I even spend hours on my phone when I am in a beautiful new country. Instead of exploring and taking in the moment, I am focused on capturing the best pictures so that my one thousand followers can see what I am doing. When really, only my grandma cares to know!

Instead, redirect your focus and energy to the real world around you. Spend your energy doing things that fuel your soul rather than meaningless social comparisons. Make a list of the things you love to do or things you have meant to do but you "haven't had time."

. . .

"We won't be distracted by comparison if we are captivated with purpose."

—Bob Goff

. . .

4. Play therapist

Ask yourself questions and analyze where your negative ideas are coming from. What can you learn from the feelings you experience when comparing yourself to others? Maybe they serve a purpose in informing you of a part of your life that needs improvement. Maybe you are feeling unworthy because someone you see online is chasing their dreams, while you are too scared to go after yours. Maybe the comparisons are reminders that you need to spend some time working on yourself so that you don't constantly measure your internal and external life to others. Use your feelings to evaluate what is really going on.

5. Avoid checking your apps as the first and last thing you do each day

If you wake up and scroll, you will stumble upon accounts that trigger the aching, gut-wrenching comparison feeling. If the last thing you do before you go to bed is analyze pictures of peoples' highlight reels, you are bound to go to bed critiquing your own life and feeling sad and anxious. Don't allow your day to start on a bad foot, and don't allow your sleep to be compromised because social media got the best of you. It's not worth it, and you won't miss out on anything, I promise.

Start your day moving your body, reading, journaling, meditating—doing whatever you need to do to feel good and grounded. A solid morning will set you up for a solid day and allow you to handle obstacles. End your day in a restorative way that centers you and embraces you with warm feelings. Read, cook, spend time with loved ones, laugh, let go of the day, and enjoy the present moment with those around you.

6. Put the phone down

Why waste your day caring what Kelly from Tri-Delt did on her Saturday night or how big Judy's birthday party was? Why compare your life to someone else's altered, posed, manipulated five-second picture?

Why spend hours of your day staring at images on a screen when you could be outside enjoying nature, having conversations with your friends, or creating something?

Put down the phone. Take a breath. And enjoy life as it is happening.

CHAPTER 4

HAPPINESS GOES WHERE HAPPINESS IS

———

"Happiness does not depend on outward conditions. It depends on inner conditions."

—DALE CARNEGIE; WRITER

It started in high school.

"When I lose ten pounds, I will wear that dress."

"I will be happy when I reach my goal weight."

"I will be happy if I get an A on this exam."

"When I get into college, then I can be happy."

Then it continued into the first two years of college.

"I'll be happy when I join a sorority."

"I can be happy when finals are over."

"I will be happy when I secure an internship."

Luckily, by my junior year of college, I realized this way of thinking was flawed.

A realization came to me as I looked back and reflected on all the years when I had worked to achieve a goal in order to be happy. All that time, when I was hyper-focused on reaching a certain goal, I said no to plans, dinners, and spontaneous adventures.

I finally shook myself and screamed: "Hey! Stop! You don't need to wait until the future to be happy! You can be happy now!"

For all of high school and through my first two years of college, my happiness was contingent on outside conditions. I pushed my happiness into the future. I believed I would only be happy once I achieved a goal. I did not focus on trying to be happy at the moment. Instead, I told myself, *no, this condition will make me happy, so I'll sacrifice my sanity now. Thanks!*

I viewed happiness as something I could "achieve" and not something that came from within, available at any time. I can't remember the exact moment when I finally understood we are in control of our happiness, that happiness is a feeling that comes from our mindset, our contentment, our gratitude. Feelings of joy, satisfaction, and fulfillment characterized happiness. But ever since, I can confidently say that I have felt freer and happier.

My view that happiness was dependent on external conditions was not something I created on my own—it was learned.

And society was my teacher.

From a young age, society teaches us that happiness is not an innate state of being. Society tells us we need to graduate from college and earn lots of money to be happy. We learn we need to look like a certain ideal in order to feel beautiful, and then we will be happy. We learn we need to find a partner, and we will live happily ever after with our two children and one dog in suburbia. We live our lives in pursuit of an ideal, but that ideal may not be true to our needs and wants. Maybe we don't want kids or marriage. Maybe we can't have kids. Maybe we want to have untraditional careers or travel the country instead of having a home base. We forget we can live our lives as we please, not as society expects us to live.

We forget happiness comes from within. We can be unconditionally happy while obviously still having typical lows at times. You do not need to push happiness to a later date or jump through hoops or change the way you are in order to be happy. Of course, you can work toward a goal that will bring you happiness, but you can also be happy *while* you are doing that work.

I have canceled plans to do homework, spending hours upon hours at the library or in my room. I have studied on Friday nights instead of going out with friends. I have woken up early on Saturdays to be the first at the library. And it was all because I told myself that if I got over 90 percent on a test or As in my classes, I would be happy. But the reality was I could have been happy the whole time, with or without those high scores. I could have worked less, enjoyed life more, and I still could have been happy and social (and most likely, I would have received the same grade). At the end of the day, getting a high score may feel good and make you happy, but that burst is short-lasting.

If your happiness is based on someone else's ideal for you or conditional on getting someone else's love and approval, what happens if their love or approval is only a fleeting moment? What happens if you never achieve your goal weight? If you never get that high salary? Will you never let yourself be happy? Or, what if you get all that you ever dreamed of? Will you be happy forever? Or will your set point readjust, and you'll experience hedonic adaptation (the tendency to return to a relatively stable, baseline level of happiness despite significant life changes)?

It is innately human to always want more. In fact, the neuroscientist Jaak Panksepp has proved it. In his studies, Panksepp found that of the seven core instincts in the human brain (fear, rage, panic, care, lust, play, and seeking), seeking is the most important (Goldhill, 2016). Panksepp explains how all mammals have this seeking system, a system linked to dopamine, the neurotransmitter for pleasure and rewards. Dopamine is part of our "wanting" system. It is not only a feel-good chemical, but it also causes you to want, desire, and seek more (Weinschenk, 2018). The connection between seeking and dopamine means that mammals are rewarded for exploring their surroundings. We get pleasure and enjoyment from looking for more.

But if we tie our happiness to the "something more" we are after, happiness will continue to be a carrot dangling from a stick in front of our face. If your happiness is tied to a goal, and you will never be fully satisfied with what you have, will you ever be happy?

HAPPINESS AND PERCEPTION

Often, what we want is out of our control, and the getting there, the wanting, the needing leads to misery and negative feelings. We push ourselves into an endless circle of "more" rather than realizing we have all that we need right now.

Wanting more in order to be happy increases discontent in the now.

Most of our unhappiness comes from perception: our perception of where we are currently, compared to where we want to be, and the gap between what we have in our present and what we think we need to have in order to be happy. The source of our unhappiness does not come from lacking the things we want, but rather it comes from our thoughts and beliefs.

Our beliefs and the stories we tell ourselves is the basis of our perception. What we believe to be true will dictate the world we see around us. If you believe things are not going well for you and everything sucks, it will. If you believe you are living your best life, you are. You are what is standing in the way of living life fully and being happy at any moment, regardless of the events surrounding you. What matters is not what you have or do not have, but your outlook. When you choose to be happy, you will be happy. When you choose not to be happy, you won't be. Happiness is a choice. Accepting where you are right now is the first step to being happy. The more you accept who you are and where you are, the happier you will become.

. . .

"You can be happy today. But instead, you choose tomorrow."

—*Marcus Aurelius*

. . .

Aurelius was one of the Roman Stoic philosophers. Stoicism is an ancient philosophy from Greece and Rome, and it is regarded as one of the most practical philosophical branches. Stoicism tries to make humans more resilient, happier, wiser, and more virtuous to make them become better parents, people, and professionals. It aims to help humans solve life problems by living with an open acceptance of events, self, and people.

Aurelius was born in 121 AD and passed away in 180 AD. For well over a thousand years, people have been pushing their happiness to a later date, denying themselves happiness today out of a belief that they will be happy tomorrow. Happiness is a choice. "You choose tomorrow," said Aurelius. Why are we choosing not to be happy? Isn't happiness the goal of life? It is for me, at least.

. . .

"The secret of happiness you see is not found in seeking more, but in developing the capacity to enjoy less."

—Socrates

. . .

I have been affected by the conditional happiness syndrome. I believed my happiness came from my achievements. I didn't allow myself to be happy as I was chasing an external source. It took me a while to understand and change my patterns, and it may for you too. I have to constantly remind myself to stay in the present moment and realize that I have all that I need right now—everything is good, right now, even when it feels like it isn't. I have to remind myself to slow down and enjoy the journey. I tend to wish my days away, hope for more, and work hard to get somewhere in the future instead of taking a deep breath and being grateful for all I have and the people I am with. I have goals, I have ambition, I want things for myself, but instead of approaching them with a sense of urgency and belief that "this will make me happy," I acknowledge that my life is already great. I already have what I need for fulfillment. Everything else I do is a bonus.

Know that deep within you, you have the capacity to feel fulfilled, confident, and calm. You have all you need. You do not need to rush to get somewhere or do something else. Right now, at this moment, you are already there. Choose to feel it.

DEBUNKING THE HAPPINESS MYTHS

The first time I took a psychology class was during my senior year of high school. Given that my high school was steps away from Harvard University's campus, we were lucky enough to have a pool of professors, authors, doctors, and intellectuals speak to our classes. On one occasion, Daniel Gilbert, a psychology professor and the author of *Stumbling on Happiness*, came to teach our class about happiness. What Dr. Gilbert really did was shock us completely.

You see, we tend to believe certain things will make us very happy. These include, but are not limited to, getting good grades, having a good job, getting married, finding a perfect relationship, losing weight, and making lots of money. But while others lead us to believe this to be true, science says otherwise.

According to scientific research, happiness is 50 percent determined by our genes, 10 percent determined by circumstances, and 40 percent determined by ourselves (Lyubomirsk, Sheldon, and Schkade, 2005). Yes, genetics do play a large role in our ultimate happiness and whether we view the glass as half full or half empty, but we are still 40 percent in control of our happiness. Science proves happiness is a choice! It is not what happens to us that affects our happiness (the 10 percent), but the story we tell in relation to our everyday experiences and circumstances. To back this up, Dr. Gilbert showed us two studies relating circumstances to happiness.

What experience could you think of that would make you extremely happy? Winning the lottery, of course! What about making you extremely unhappy? Maybe losing the ability to use your limbs.

Well, in a 1978 study, the researchers Brickman, Coates, and Janoff-Bulman studied relative happiness in twenty-two lottery winners, twenty-two controls, and twenty-nine paraplegics. The results concluded that "a year after losing the use of their legs, and a year after winning the lotto, lottery winners and paraplegics are equally happy with their lives." Years later researchers found the paraplegics were less happy than the lottery winners, but the difference was not as stark as you would think. We would also assume lottery winners would be happier years later, but in actuality, they just adapted and created a new baseline for their happiness. The 10 percent really didn't affect happiness. Both groups just adapted to their circumstances and experienced hedonic adaptation.

What else did Dr. Gilbert debunk that day? Money and happiness. We assume the more money we have, the fewer problems we have, and the happier we will be. But as The Notorious B.I.G. stated, "mo money mo problems." Having more money does not necessarily buy more happiness. Danny Kahneman and Angus Deaton, psychologists and economists who won a Nobel prize in economics, wrote a famous paper analyzing the correlation between money and happiness in Americans. In 2008–2009, Kahneman and Deaton studied 450,000 Americans, looking at the relationship between their income and their happiness. To study the correlation, Kahneman and Deaton used reported measures of positive affect (smiling, happiness, enjoyment), not blue (not reporting worry or sadness), and feeling stress-free. They found happiness does positively increase with higher incomes, but after around $75,000, there is no longer an increase in happiness at higher salaries. It seems that $75,000 is the threshold at which further increases in income no longer improve individuals' happiness and subjective well-being. Bill Gates, Kim Kardashian, and Taylor Swift are no happier because of their finances than someone who earns $75,000. The difference in happiness after that is in your control and preset by your genetics.

In the book *The American Paradox* by David Myers, Myers wrote, "Our becoming much better off over the last four decades has not been accompanied by one iota of increased subjective well-being." All the extra stuff we think we need is not making us happier!

Another happiness myth that threw me for a loop (and one I personally know to be true): there is no evidence that weight loss is associated with improved psychological well-being. In fact, a study found the opposite. In 2014, Jackson et al., released a study that surveyed two thousand obese individuals on a diet program. The participants all followed the same diet program and were surveyed over a four-year period. Prior to the program, the individuals believed losing weight would make them happier. However, four years later, researchers found those who lost weight reported a more depressed mood than those who remained stable or had gained weight. Losing weight didn't make them happy. It made them more unhappy—just as it did for me!

And finally, perfect grades. Have you ever felt like you totally crushed a test but later got the grades back and realized you did poorly or failed? I have in my junior year of college, managerial accounting (yikes). We would predict this would make us sad, but does it? Levine et al., conducted a study in 2012 on grades. The study used undergraduates enrolled in an introductory psychology course at the University of California, Irvine, as their participants. Two weeks prior to receiving their exam grade, students in the class were asked to predict their happiness based on their grade being higher than expected, lower than expected, or as expected. Two weeks later, students received their exam grades, and researchers followed up a few days later to measure their actual happiness levels. They found in reality, your happiness does not go as high as you would expect for good grades, and it does not go as low for lower grades. Happiness levels are about equal regardless of the grade. All in all, grades do not impact your happiness as much as you would think.

Scientists, philosophers, psychologists, and economists all agree: For the most part, it is not what you have or don't have that makes you happy. It is your view on what you have that makes you happy.

If you keep making your happiness conditional and continue viewing happiness as being tied to something, you will be disappointed and miss out on being happy now. Happiness does not have to be conditional. It never did. Allow yourself to be happy now and happy at any stage—happy even if things aren't going as planned, and happy when they are. You do not need something to be happy. You do not need someone to be happy. You do not need to tie your happiness to others' opinions of you. All you need to be happy is you. And you deserve to be happy.

A CHALLENGE FOR YOU:

Write down everything you think you have needed to be, do, accomplish, or have in order to be happy—a list of things society taught you, things you thought for yourself, or things imposed on you from other parts of your life. Once you have that list, cross out all the conditions. Cross out the "I will be happy when," "I can be happy if," "When I have... I can be happy." You can leave it at that or go a step further by writing "I am in control of my happiness and my life. Happiness is an innate state of being and not something I need to achieve" next to each condition. Or replace the things you need with the things that you are already lucky to have and make you happy right now.

Having lots of money ≠ Happiness

Working on something you love and are passionate about = Happiness

Being skinny ≠ Happiness

Taking care of your body and loving the way you look as you are = Happiness

Being famous ≠ Happiness

Sharing your love of your craft with the world = Happiness

Having a big party, wedding, etc. ≠ Happiness

Spending time with the ones you love = Happiness

Living in a huge house ≠ Happiness

Living with people you love = Happiness

Owning lots of material things ≠ Happiness

Giving = Happiness

PART TWO:

LOVE

CHAPTER 5

YOU ARE YOUR MOST IMPORTANT RELATIONSHIP

———

"Owning our story and loving ourselves through that process is the bravest thing that we'll ever do."

—BRENÉ BROWN; RESEARCHER AND AUTHOR

For years I couldn't love myself without praise from others. I needed admiration, acceptance—anything that could make me feel good about who I am and what I do. I worked my butt off in school so I could make good grades and get certificates. I attended an academically rigorous college so that people would say things like, "Wow, you must be smart, that's a good school." I spent way too long on homework assignments and studying for exams in the hopes my hard work would pay off—obtaining an "A" warranted congratulations, and "That's fantastic, I am so proud." The more As, the more cheer. I ran a half marathon because I wanted to stand out from my peers. I ate extremely healthily and disciplined so that people would applaud me for my self-control and dedication. I worked out six to seven times a week because I wanted both the body people would compliment and the acknowledgment of my motivation and strength. I jumped at any opportunity that would result in praise. I needed it because I couldn't give it to myself.

The problem was not my goals. It was my intention behind them.

Since I grew into my womanly body at the ripe age of eleven and started to compare my accomplishments and physical being to the world around me and on my phone screen, I have never felt like I was good enough or I had done enough. I am a part of the statistic that "Seven in ten girls believe they are not good enough or don't measure up in some way, including their looks, performance in school and relationships with friends and family members" (Shapiro, 2014). I am the rule rather than the exception.

How could I love or even like myself if I constantly saw others achieve more, look fitter, dress cuter, laugh louder, be prettier than I was? I couldn't love myself if others didn't give me a reason to. I didn't know how. If someone told me I was pretty, then I was pretty until they would stop, and then I had to do something else to get their attention. I regarded others approval and opinion of me as more important than my own. I subconsciously told them, "Your view of me, which can change day by day and change depending on how you are feeling right now, is more important than my own opinion of myself." I cared deeply about what other people thought of me. I lived to satisfy other's demands, points of view, needs, desires.

It was as if they had brought me flowers, but I needed to learn to grow them on my own.

"I AM NOT WHAT I DO"

In the sixth grade, my best friend, Lina, and I were falling behind in school. This was probably because we sat next to each other in every class and spent most of the time doodling or passing notes back and forth. When we received our report cards for the first quarter, my heart sank at the low grades I had received. It was the first report card I ever got, and it was definitely not what I wanted to see. I automatically started thinking I was a failure, I wasn't "smart enough," and I would never be good at school. So, when Lina turned to me at lunch the next day and said, "Why don't we go to performing arts school instead?" My first reaction was, "That's a great idea!" If I couldn't be good at school and get the accolades I desired there, I would switch schools and try my hand at being an actress.

After weeks of honing my dance skills, perfecting my three-minute monologue, and attempting to sound like a half-decent singer, our moms accompanied Lina and me as we hopped on the train to London to audition for the Arts Educational Schools London.

Two weeks after our audition, we both received a phone call of our acceptance. Lina chose to take her placement, but I declined mine.

While we were waiting on our admission decisions, I started doing better in school, seeing my grades go up, and although I loved acting, I didn't want to jump into the career at twelve years old. The only reason I pursued the idea was because I was defined by my accomplishments. If I couldn't do well in school, I had to chase something else, something I was good at—something that would garner acclaim.

Even at twelve years old, I had slipped into the notion and belief that "I am what I do." That I am my accomplishments, but I am also my failures. It was not until later in life, sitting at the dinner table, when my dad complimented my mom's cooking, and she responded, "Thank you, but I am not my cooking," when I realized I am not what I do. We are all not what we do. My mom isn't what she cooks, whether her food tastes good (which it usually does, a benefit of having a mom who used to own a catering company) or whether her food isn't so tasty. Even if you end up disliking this book, which I really hope you don't, I am not my book. Yes, these are my thoughts, my beliefs, but I am so much more than the words I am writing.

I have spent twenty-two years walking on a tight rope between a win and a loss, always anxious that even if I was winning, I would accidentally slip up, fall, and fail. Even to this day, I struggle with the balancing act and slipping into the notion that "I am what I do." When I stop and remind myself, "I am not my cooking," I realize it doesn't matter if I "win" or "lose." I am me, and I am doing the best I can.

WHEN WE FOCUS ON WHAT WE DON'T HAVE, WE CAN'T ENJOY WHAT WE ALREADY DO HAVE

For much of high school, negative feelings clouded my thoughts toward my body and myself. There wasn't any mental space to think about anything else. I didn't know what I wanted to do with my life. I didn't know which college I wanted to attend. I didn't have any hobbies I was interested in pursuing. I was so stuck in life because I was so focused on thinking about what I didn't have rather than what I did have. I focused on the lack: the body I didn't have, the grades I didn't achieve, the trophies I didn't win. The more time I spent zoned in on what I didn't have, the less I was able to attract abundance into my life. I hardly ever spent time thinking of all the blessings around me.

I took my family for granted, never fully appreciating their support for whatever I wanted to do, including dropping out of school to pursue acting with no experience. I had traveled to many different countries and learned about different cultures and ways of life. I lived near a city with endless people to meet, activities to do, and things to explore. I had family and friends who loved me. I was healthy. I lived in a warm home with everything I could need. We always had a full fridge.

If for one moment I started taking inventory of all the amazing things I had in my life, things I was grateful for, I am sure I would have seen I was living a great life and already had so much. I didn't need more.

BREAKING THE FLAWED THOUGHT PATTERN TO MAKE PEACE WITH YOURSELF

My thinking was fundamentally flawed, which widened the gap between me and my ability to love myself. I was flawed in four ways:

1. I cared more about what others thought of me than my own opinion
2. I defined myself by my accomplishments and my failures
3. I tied who I am as a person to the way I look
4. I was fixated on what I didn't possess

All four of these thought patterns were standing in the way of me embracing myself and appreciating what I have. In order to start the process of finding love within myself, I had to recognize my flawed thinking, break the old pattern, and forgive myself. I had to allow myself to be human, to make mistakes, to be vulnerable, to not have everything figured out, and to not have to do everything. I had to allow myself to just be as I am and make peace with her.

During my last year in college, I was not in a good mental place. I spent hours alone in my room huddled on my computer screen, trying to take hard college classes while having an "I'm about to have all these responsibilities after graduating and have no idea where to start" crisis. On multiple occasions, I curled my body into the fetal position as I cried to my mom on the phone, pleading to come home. My mom and her advice is kind of like a chocolate-vanilla swirled ice cream: the vanilla side is her nurture and loving energy, while her chocolate side is a mix of wise words and hard-hitting truth. Sometimes you get the vanilla, sometimes the chocolate, or sometimes a mix of both. Somehow it is always what you need to hear. One day when I was having another breakdown, I got the perfect mix of vanilla and chocolate.

"Mom, I need to come home. I am so unhappy here; I want to be there." To which she replied, "Livia, come home whenever you need, we will support you in whatever you choose, but I want you to know that wherever you go, there you are. You cannot run away from your problems, especially if your problems are within you. If you want to come, please make sure it is not because you are trying to run and hide because if you come here, they will follow."

My mom quoted Jon Kabat-Zinn when she said, "Wherever you go, there you are." It was exactly what I needed to hear, and I think about it often. If you're not at peace with yourself, escaping to a new place, buying a new outfit, winning a game, making lots of money, chasing after some external thing—those things—will not fix that. I had to do the inner work. I had to spend time practicing self-love, rewiring my thoughts, and replacing the flawed thought patterns with self-compassion. I had to remind myself that at the end of the day, I am the only person who will be with me through everything: heartbreak, grief, happiness, ups, downs, ebbs, flows. No one will know what it is like to be me or how it feels to live in my body and see things the way I do. If I had the option, I would want my best friend, teammate, and biggest supporter to be with me through everything. And I could have that. I could learn to be my own biggest supporter, my own companion.

SELF-LOVE IS A RELATIONSHIP WITH ONESELF

I started to love myself slowly as I started to build a relationship with myself. Like any relationship, your relationship with yourself takes time to grow, time to nurture, and requires effort and attention. In relationships, there will be periods of excitement and fun, as well as periods of conflict and heartache. It is through the deep and often difficult work of growing and working through problems that connections grow, and love gets stronger.

I had to treat myself like I would a close friend, family member, or partner. If someone close to me is going through a hard time, I don't bring them down further and start nit-picking their being. I treat them with respect. I give them compassion, kindness, and patience. I had to give myself the same grace I give to those I love. I had to say to myself, "You're doing the best you can, and that is all I ask." As Maya Angelou once said: "Do the best you can until you know better. When you know better, do better." Doing the best you can is not slacking.

It's releasing unattainable high standards and replacing them with the promise to continue to grow as you learn. It's freeing yourself from needing to be "perfect" and to just do what you can do with where you are at.

Self-love meant putting less pressure on trying to please others and more emphasis on pleasing myself. It meant listening to my needs, my wants, my desires, my point of view, and caring more about how I view myself than how others view me. If I am able to believe in myself, to enjoy the person I am, to see the incredible person that I can become, anything is possible.

I had to overcome self-doubt to build my confidence. Confidence is about trust, reputation, and held promises. It is about consistently keeping promises to yourself, knowing when you say you are going to do something, you do it. A lot of self-love and self-confidence comes from learning to trust yourself. I started to keep the promises I made to myself: the promise to go to the gym after school, the promise to go to bed early, the promise to eat healthily, the promise to read every day. The more promises I kept, the better my reputation became with myself, the more I was able to trust myself.

Self-confidence is a process. Just like any new skill, the more you are able to practice, the stronger your confidence muscle grows. When I became more confident, I pushed myself to apply to the jobs, the schools, the internships that I wanted. I didn't doubt my capabilities or hold myself back. I believed I would end up where I needed to and had trust in my abilities to do the work when I got there.

Every day I try to practice the three elements of self-compassion Brené Brown outlines in her book *The Gifts of Imperfection*.

1. Self-kindness: Being loving and understanding toward ourselves when we suffer, fail, or feel inadequate—replacing self-criticism and judgment with warmth and care.

   - Self-kindness can be practiced anytime you start to feel negative about yourself. Let's say, for instance, you fail a test. Instead of feeding yourself with judgmental and critical thoughts, stop, take a deep breath, and replace the negative beliefs with understanding and supportive ones. Telling yourself: "It is okay, it was one test. It means nothing about how smart or capable you are." Self-kindness is about being your own loving and supportive friend.

2. Humanity: We all go through hard things. Suffering, insecurities, and feelings of inadequacy are part of what it means to be human. Perfection does not exist.

   - The next time you feel inadequate or insecure, gently remind yourself that everyone at one time or another feels this way. It is completely okay and normal to feel shame and sorrow. In fact, at times you are down, there are hundreds, if not millions, of other people feeling the same way, at the same time. We are all human, doing the best we can, going through many of the same ups and downs. It is all going to be okay.

3. Mindfulness: "We cannot ignore our pain and feel compassion for it at the same time." Mindfulness is about noticing and allowing our emotions to be what they are. It is about not suppressing or exaggerating them, rather just sitting and observing them as they flow through.

   - Whenever you have a thought or feeling, just sit back and observe. You are allowed to have your feelings and to feel any emotion you have. But don't assign any label to them, critique them, judge yourself for having them, let them be as they are.

Little reminders every day to be more self-compassionate, more trusting, and kinder help me redirect my negative thoughts and treat myself as a friend. It helps me further strengthen my relationship with myself and see I am worthy and enough as I am. It helps me to be able to control my emotions. To be able to soak in the good moments and be gentle with myself during the bad. To find the courage to live as I am.

My journey of self-love will never be complete. It's a daily practice, a life-long process, not a destination. But through the years, the practice has been easier, and I am in a much better place. I wish giving yourself love was as easy as giving it to a friend or loved one. It's not easy, but with time and practice, it gets easier, and you'll find your own special tricks and techniques that help you get back to a place of self-compassion and respect.

HOW TO START BUILDING A STRONG RELATIONSHIP WITH YOURSELF:

1. Honesty

The truth can sometimes be a hard pill to swallow, but it allows us to move forward. When we know the truth, we can start to make the changes, to become stronger, to learn and grow from there. In order for me to start learning to love myself, I had to be honest with myself. I had to develop a new sense of self-awareness for the reasons why I did the things I did. Did I do those things for myself or someone else? Why did I work so hard for good grades? Why did I feel like a failure when I didn't do so well? I had to take the time and space to get to know my choices and my thought patterns. Once I understood myself more, I was able to start working on the areas that needed healing. I was able to recognize moments when I was overly critical of myself, and instead, take a deep breath, extend compassion, and try to be loving

Be honest with yourself. Where is your thinking flawed? What prevents you from loving and trusting yourself? What areas need work? Ask yourself the hard questions. Reflect on your past, your hurts and hurdles, and times when you felt your best. Who was there? What were you doing? What was said? How did you feel? Take time to reflect and become self-aware—this is half the work.

Denial often comes into play here. We don't like thinking of the parts of us that need work. Denial is a powerful self-sabotaging behavior that keeps us stuck where we are, continuing the behaviors that hold us back. To overcome and move past denial, we need to be brutally honest with ourselves, so we can express all of our emotions and fears. We need to understand the potential consequences of our actions and what could happen if we don't make a change. I personally overcame denial by releasing my feelings and thoughts. For so long, I kept them locked away in my head and heart, which made denial easy. When I opened the lock and let them out, either through journaling or talking to someone I trusted, I could no longer deny the truth, and I had to confront what was holding me back.

2. Respect
A huge part of any relationship is having respect for your partner. Respect is about accepting someone as they are, no matter what they do, think, or believe. It is knowing your

partner may be different than you are, have different experiences, and points of view, and that is okay. When we respect one another, we allow each other to come as we are and feel safe being ourselves.

In the relationship you are building with yourself, self-respect is important. When we respect ourselves, we believe we are enough, that we deserve to be treated well, and we are worthy. Self-respect is about understanding who we are, what we believe in, what our values are. When we have self-respect, we can establish boundaries, stand up for ourselves, and not let anyone treat us poorly. Self-respect correlates with the inner dialogue we all carry with ourselves every day. If our inner dialogue is critical and judgmental, you might want to look at how you are respecting yourself. For example, you miss a train and are late to meet a friend for coffee. A healthy inner dialogue may look like this: "I am going to let my friend know I missed the train, and I will treat her to a coffee once I arrive." An unhealthy inner dialogue may look like this: "I always do this. I am the worst friend and can never get to things on time." The way we speak to ourselves is extremely important. It has a huge impact on who we become and what we do. If we speak to ourselves with care, we can start to become our own best friend and see all the amazing qualities we possess.

It takes time to develop. It is a quality that comes from within and, through inner work, can be strengthened. But when you have it, when you have self-respect and know who you are, you will no longer need others' approval to know you are good enough. Because you are, you always are, worthy and enough. You just might not fully feel it yet.

3. Forgiveness

Forgive yourself. We all make mistakes, we all carry some form of regret, we all have moments we wish we could have changed what we said or the way we acted. Making mistakes and doing things "wrong" is a part of being human. We need to make mistakes in order to grow. Most of my learning experiences have come from me making a mistake. My mistakes have taught me an invaluable lesson that allowed me to grow, mature, and become a better person. I don't wish I could go back and redo anything because the lesson learned was worth my emotional pain from my wrongdoings.

It is unfair to judge your past self for what you now know. It is unfair to be angry with yourself for things out of your control. Holding onto anger, bitterness, resentment, any negative emotion is a waste of energy. Forgive yourself, grow, and channel that energy to working toward self-acceptance.

4. Acceptance

You are you.

You cannot be anyone else but yourself.

And guess what?

The odds of you being you and being born are one in four hundred trillion (Robbins, 2011).

I will say it again for emphasis, *one in four hundred trillion*. We are all literal walking miracles. The fact that you were born, when you were, to the parents you were, as you are, is pretty incredible. Although I know we sometimes wish we were someone else, looked different, had more opportunities growing up, whatever it may be. You are you, and you are you for a reason.

It is okay, and completely normal, to not love or even like many parts about yourself. But we can still not love everything about us and accept ourselves as we are. Self-acceptance is embracing who we are—embracing our circumstances, our families, our genetics, our life choices. When we accept this is the life we are blessed with, we work with it rather than against it.

It has taken me twenty-two years to finally accept and embrace who I am. To accept that the body I have wants to be curvy, and I will never be a 5'10, size zero model. To accept that although there are many things I might never be able to do because of my genetics, talents, and abilities, there are still a plethora of things I can do.

When I accepted who I am, I opened my eyes to the potential, possibilities, and opportunities I have rather than wishing I was someone else or focusing on all the things I can't do. I no longer tried to make my body fit clothes. Rather I found clothes that fit my body—the size didn't matter anymore, the way I felt did. I no longer spent my days focused on what I didn't have, what I didn't like, the lack. I spent my days doing things I enjoyed, no matter what they were. I no longer looked in the mirror and pointed out everything I didn't like. I accepted what I saw and either made amends or made a change. I made peace with who I am, and instead of trying to change her, I am trying to make her a happier, kinder person.

Honesty, respect, forgiveness, and acceptance are not all you need to build a relationship, but they are a good start.

Your relationship with yourself is a journey, not a destination. Some parts of the journey will be smooth sailing. Other points will be bumpy, rocky, and sometimes scary. I promise it is worth the work.

As you grow closer to yourself, as you begin to embrace and love your special gifts and unique being, you'll become more powerful. You'll shine brighter, laugh louder, love harder, dream bigger. You will be able to step fully into your life and live a truer version of what it means to be you. Not only will you be better off, but the world around you will also be too because you will be able to share your gift with the world—the gift that is you.

CHAPTER 6

BE THE MAIN CHARACTER IN YOUR LIFE

_____

"Nothing happens unless first we dream."

—CARL SANDBURG; POET

If you were to write a book right now, with you as the main character and no plot off-limits, what would you want to write?

I walk down the street, the wind lightly lifting my red midi dress, so it dances softly in the air. I dodge past tourists idly walking and avoid the other professionals who are too focused on their iPhones to notice me. My black Celine bag hangs off my shoulder. My manicured nails grip the straps, so I don't lose any of the contents. Today is the day I have been waiting for since moving to DC a year ago. Today is the day I sign my book deal and embrace opportunities to travel the world to inspire women to live their lives the way they want to and learn to love who they are. Today is my day.

I approach my destination, the boutique Line Hotel in Adams Morgan. The building, once a church, sits high and mighty. Just beyond the columns and the heavy doors is a bustling atmosphere, a beautiful interior, and Dan, the man with the important papers. My curled hair tickles my shoulders as a cocktail of nerves and excitement overtakes my body. I ascend the steps, careful not to trip on my dress, even though by this point, I'm a professional at wearing heels. I walk into the lobby, and as I have imagined since I first got the phone call, there he is, grinning at me with a stack of papers on the small round table in front of him. I stop, taking in the moment, making sure my memory doesn't miss any detail. I take in the scent of coffee and freshly baked croissants. I take in the people in the middle of the lobby, lounging on the black leather couches typing away on their laptops. I take in the autumn breeze that brushes against my back as the door opens and closes behind me. I almost pinch myself—is this a dream?

Wow, I am only a few signatures away from having everything I wanted since moving to DC. I have my dream job as an event planner and soon-to-be motivational speaker/author. I live in my dream city. At home, my family and best friends anticipate popping the champagne to celebrate. Life is good.

This the beginning of my dream story, starring me. Sad to say, I am currently at my parents' house in Cambridge, Massachusetts, sitting on a couch in my black sweats—not in a pretty red dress. But one day, it will happen because I'll make sure of it.

WE GET TO WRITE THE PLOT

We should dream about the life we want and the people we want in it. We should fantasize about the job, the apartment, the house, the city, the partner, the fun. We should picture our lives like a novel, one for which we write the plot, and we are the protagonist. One where we get to turn the page when things aren't working out the way we want them to and start fresh. Where we can edit our beliefs about our potential and expand the image of who we are to become, what the best version of ourselves looks like. We are allowed to enjoy our lives and to make them the way we want. We are allowed to put ourselves first and go after our vision. We are allowed to be the main character in our books and in our lives.

How would you answer the question I asked at the beginning of this chapter? What adventures would your character experience, and who would be the other featured character? How does your protagonist act? How do they treat others? How do they treat themselves? Stop right now and think about it, maybe even write it down. Without any barriers and "that could never happen," what is the story you want to tell? How do you wish your life will unfold?

Hold onto that vision, don't let it go, because I have a secret for you:

· · ·

"If you are still looking for that one person who will change your life, take a look in the mirror."

—Roman Price

· · ·

We cannot just imagine our lives were a certain way and watch it immediately change. Unfortunately, we don't have a fairy godmother for that one. It's up to you. You are responsible for your life and how you feel living it. Every day, at any moment, you have a new opportunity to make a change, to start the page afresh. If you want more for your life or to change your life's direction, know that it can happen for you. But also know that no path is easier than the other. There will always be ups and downs. Spending every day wishing you were someone else or doing something else is difficult. Changing that lifestyle is also difficult. You have to choose which path you want to take.

No matter where you come from, how much money you have, the people in your life, take solace in knowing you are never stuck. There is always a way out and always a new path to explore.

WISHING DOESN'T GET YOU ANYWHERE

Bronnie Ware, a palliative nurse in Australia, has spent many years working with patients at the end of their lives. In her book, *The Top Five Regrets of the Dying,* Ware recounts her conversations with dying patients. She notes there were five recurring themes when asking patients if they had any regrets or would have done anything differently. The most common answer was, "I wish I'd had the courage to live a life true to myself, not the life others expected of me."

Too many people get to the end of the road only realizing they had so much life to live but spent too much of it on others' dimes. As the Dalai Lama Tenzin Gyatso so eloquently said, "Man. Because he sacrifices his health in order to make money. He sacrifices money to recuperate his health. And then he is so anxious about the future he does not enjoy the present. The result being he does not live in the present or the future. He lives as if he is never going to die, and then dies having never really lived."

You are not here to please everybody. You are not here to conform to society's ideals for what makes a man or woman good or bad. You are not here to live your life the way others think you should. Whether it be the person you fall in love with, the unconventional job you want, the desire to quit your job and travel the world, you are here to live your life your way—to grow more into the person you want to be and build a life and a future that makes sense and feels good to you. If you need to disappoint someone, make sure that person isn't you.

FOLLOW YOUR ENTHUSIASM

American journalist, former Editor-in-Chief of *Teen Vogue*, *New York Times* best-selling author of *More Than Enough*, and the newest judge of *Project Runway* are just some of the caps that Elaine Welteroth wears.

Having served as the youngest Editor-in-Chief of *Teen Vogue* and being a go-getter by nature, Elaine is someone who embodies what it means to have passions, dreams, and to be unstoppable.

All of her life, Elaine was fascinated by the world of media. While many little kids play make-believe house or princess, unbeknownst to Elaine and her family, Elaine's make-believe was practice for her future. Elaine's bath times turned into her own personal talk show where she was both the interviewee and the interviewer—already finding the perfect way to get all the gossip and behind-the-scenes secrets. By the time she was eight years old, Elaine and her best friend were entrepreneurs in training, creating their own magazine using construction paper and Saran Wrap to get the ideal glossy feel for their pages. And all through her childhood, at exactly 4:00 p.m. Monday through Friday, Elaine watched

The Oprah Winfrey Show, spending years learning how to tell authentic stories.

Even though it is clear from her childhood that Elaine was meant for the world of media, she didn't fully trust that it was for her until her senior year of college.

In an interview for Ashley Graham's Podcast *Pretty Big Deal*, Elaine tells Ashley, "Once I figured out what I wanted to do. I had blinders on. Nothing could stop me."

During the fall semester of senior year, Elaine finally set her sights on pursuing a career in the magazine world. Believing that once she got her foot in the door, she could climb the ladder and, one day, make it to the top as editor-in-chief.

Elaine stopped at nothing to make her dream come true. Although her go-getter nature started as a child, creating beauty salon and magazine businesses with her best friends, Elaine's first real push started when she applied for internships postgraduation.

It started when Elaine read an article on Alicia Keys written by someone named Harriette Cole. Elaine had never heard of Ms. Cole, but her brilliant words led Elaine to type "Harriette Cole" into an internet search bar. Looking back at Elaine was a headshot of a confident Black woman with a bio that made Elaine's heart flutter with excitement. Harriette had an impressive resume. She had previously worked at *Essence* magazine for eleven years, eventually working her way up to fashion director, after which she made a brave leap and started her own production company, Harriette Cole Media. Ms. Cole also holds the title of bestselling author, motivational speaker, and mother. At the time of Elaine's Google search, Harriette held the position of creative director and Editor-in-Chief of *EBONY* magazine. With her long and thriving career across multiple media platforms, Harriette was someone Elaine knew she could learn a lot from as she was the quintessence of someone Elaine strove to become (Welteroth, 2019).

Although Elaine had just sent off her internship application to *Essence* magazine, a magazine that Elaine had idolized since she was a young girl, something within Elaine called for her to reach out to Harriette.

Elaine spent weeks drafting and editing the perfect introduction email, sending it by snail mail and email. Continuously calling Harriette's office to see if they received her email, stopping at nothing until she got just ten minutes of her time. And even when phone calls went unanswered or rejected, she kept pushing. "Every day, I would call and just beg her for time with Harriette," Elaine shared during a radio interview with *The Breakfast Club*. She claimed she would tell Harriette's assistant she would bring Harriette a coffee, despite living across the country.

Elaine was willing to fly from California to New York just to share a coffee with Harriette. Now that is serious dedication.

After graduation, Elaine received the email that she received acceptance into *Essence*'s 2008 intern class. Her dreams of moving to New York to work at her dream company came true right before her eyes. But exactly thirty days before she boarded a flight to New York, Elaine finally got a phone call from Harriette.

Harriette asked Elaine to work at a cover shoot for *Ebony*. The shoot was in California, and they were in need of a local production assistant. Elaine jumped for joy and enthusiastically said, "Yes!"

The cover shoot was for Serena Williams, adding a cherry on the cake to Elaine's day. But the real cake came at the end of the shoot after Elaine had impressed everyone. Sitting down with Harriette as the shoot wrapped, Harriette smiled at Elaine and said, "You are hired... We'll start with a summer internship. And then we will go from there" (Welteroth, 2019).

Even though Elaine planned to intern at *Essence*, Elaine could not turn down the opportunity to work under Harriette at *Ebony*. A few days later, Elaine called *Essence* to decline her position, despite it being a bigger, more "glamorous" magazine. Elaine knew by taking the opportunity with *Ebony*, she would be able to work closely with the higher-ups and have more of an impact. Telling Ashley Graham on her podcast: "Don't chase the sexy... At the end of the day, you are the one who has to come home to yourself. You are the one who has to get up every day and go back to work. The work has to be fulfilling enough. You can't do it for the hope of impressing other people or getting accolades. It has to be intrinsically satisfying."

Come fall, Elaine had managed to stay with *Ebony* and even earned herself a raise.

Eventually, Elaine worked her way up from *Ebony* to *Glamour* to *Teen Vogue* as the first Black beauty director in Conde Nast's history.

She made her dreams come true and more.

How did she do it?

She worked hard for it. She went above and beyond in her duties. She asked for the raises, for the coffee chats, for the meetings. She didn't stop. She kept her dream in front of her mind and looked for opportunities, sometimes even creating the opportunities.

Even with the no's, the unanswered emails and phone calls, being left at a networking lunch because she was "too young," Elaine kept her head up and her eye on the prize.

When Ashley asked her how she did it all, how she made her choices of where to go and what to do, Elaine said: "Follow your enthusiasm, your mind can play tricks on you, and your heart can change."

And that is what I want you to know.

It does not matter how big or small your dreams are.

It does not matter if you do not currently have the networks or opportunities.

It does not matter if you started off down one career path and now want to do a one-eighty.

It can happen.

Just keep following your enthusiasm.

YOU CAN MAKE IT HAPPEN

Going forward, I urge you to do a few things.

1. Start writing a draft of your story

Start dreaming of the life you want and start visualizing the person you want to be. Think about the identity you want to have, the qualities, beliefs, and how you give to others. Think about the kind of people you would want in your life, the career, the country, the hobbies, the talents.

Some chapters have already written themselves. You have already lived those years. Use the past chapters as inspiration or motivation for the chapters and years to come.

2. As the main character, who do you want to be?

Ask yourself, "What kinds of things would this person start doing?" Would they start volunteering, or would they read every day? Would they start deepening their friendships or look for opportunities to expand their network? Make a list of the things they do.

3. Reflect on your past

Think about the times you felt best. What were the circumstances and the types of activities you were doing? How were you taking care of yourself and others? Taking those into account, what are some ways for you to recharge? What kinds of activities leave you feeling centered, grounded, refreshed?

Maybe by reflecting on your past, you will realize that, similarly to Elaine, you grew up with clear passions and interests that you have yet to fully explore.

4. How can you go from here

Looking down at what you have written, decide and start now. What is the next right move that will bring you closer to who you want to be? It's never too late to start.

I may not be walking down the streets of DC in a red midi dress or carrying a Celine bag (those things are expensive)! But that doesn't mean it won't be my reality one day. Until then, I am going to keep dreaming, keep imagining the fun outfits, the outrageously expensive bags that, let's be honest, might not be in my future. Keep picturing more for myself and working toward that every day. I'll sit in my sweatpants until one day I'll be gallivanting in my heels.

CHAPTER 7

THANK YOU... NEXT ONE!

—————

"When someone shows you who they are, believe them the first time."

—MAYA ANGELOU; CIVIL RIGHTS ACTIVIST AND POET

The sun brightly shined, as summer was in full swing. Junior year of high school just ended, and I was sitting outside on the screened-in porch enjoying the sun while simultaneously trying to protect my pale skin. The newly redecorated porch quickly became my favorite place in my house. Around me, as I sat on the blue sectional couch—that was a tad too big for the space, in my opinion—were twinkle lights that cascaded down the sides of the walls swinging gently in the warm breeze, a coffee table overtaken with all my necessities for the afternoon, a speaker in the corner that my favorite music danced out of, and long billowy white curtains which lined the windows, hanging just right to make this space my own little oasis. The afternoon light was peeking through the curtains. I sighed as a Taylor Swift song came on. While it instantly put me in my feelings, it also reminded me about the lack of romance in my life.

My mom was washing dishes in the kitchen as I went through the door and plopped on the barstool, "Ugh, Mom, I want a boyfriend to hang out with on the porch." Without hesitation or direct eye contact, she responded with: "Ask the universe, then let it go. You are in a great place, and it will come when it does."

Until that point, I had never been religious or spiritual, but I did know a little about the law of attraction, mostly because of my mom. I thought to myself, *Hey, there's no harm in taking that advice.*

So right then and there, I asked the universe for the first time: "Hey universe, I know I haven't talked to you before, but I would really like a boyfriend to sit outside on the porch with— thanks!" I said my piece, let the idea go, and then hopped off the stool and went back outside to continue listening to some good music.

Later that evening, my parents and I went to dinner to celebrate the end of junior year. Immersed in a great conversation over what we would be making for brunch the next morning, prior to us even eating dinner, I might add, my phone buzzed in my lap. I pulled my napkin off to reveal a text message that read, "Hey, do you want to go to dinner and the movies next weekend?"

Boom, drop the mic. The universe has spoken.

That text was from a boy in my AP calculus class. He was tall, cute, and a senior. He was charming, and everyone liked him, including me. We had just been assigned seats next to each other in class for the last month, and I had a crush on him, but I knew nothing would happen. It was the second semester. We were friends. He was outgoing, cute, athletic, and did I mention cute? I was insecure, shy, and a junior. But he just asked *me* out.

Trying not to seem too eager, I waited a bit before responding. "Yeah, sure, sounds fun." It was a response that admittedly took me way too long to come up with.

That text led to a slew of late-night hangouts on the aforementioned porch until 3 or 4 a.m. as we talked about everything; no topic was off-limits. It led to multiple nights driving on the highway listening to loud music and singing at the top of our lungs. To flowers and cupcakes at my doorstep on my first day of senior year. Chocolate pretzels when I came back from a doctor's appointment. A spontaneous three-hour drive to Maine to meet my whole family, with flowers and chocolates in tow. A surprise visit for my birthday. And many sweet notes on my bed. It led to a first relationship that sounded beautiful and like a cheesy rom-com. In all honesty, it was pretty on the outside and empty on the inside.

The beginning was the picture-perfect honeymoon phase, filled with the "sweet" moments mentioned above. I was absolutely smitten and captivated by his charm. But a few months in, around October, warning signs and obvious red flags were blaring in my face. It started when he admitted to only dating me in the beginning because he wanted a girlfriend. I was originally his "filler girlfriend." Yep, that's right. I was supposed to be a placeholder until he found someone he *actually* liked—what a blow to the ego. My heart immediately sank into my stomach. Here I thought, *Wow, this boy likes me and wants to date me!* When in reality, I was just a pawn in his game. I had to take a deep breath and fake a tight lip smile not to show how sad that comment made me. Meanwhile, he had a big smile on his face like I was supposed to be extremely happy that over the past six months, he ended up *actually* liking me. Wow, thanks dude, I feel great about myself. That was the first warning sign I paid attention to; there were way more before that, but I chose to overlook the prior because c-h-o-c-o-l-a-t-e p-r-e-t-z-e-l-s.

The next red flag was when he told my mom and me over dinner that he thought "lying was okay if it brings the other person joy." This was after he told us a story from his past weekend where he lied about living in Amsterdam to impress a photographer he was working with. He seemed so okay with lying to get ahead, which made me think: "What else could he be covering up?" I kept quiet the rest of dinner. Once he left, my mom brought it up because it was extremely concerning. I told her I was also uncomfortable and that it went against my values. And yet, I continued to stay with him for six more months because having a boyfriend was a coveted position, and I wasn't about to give that up. I ignored my gut, my values, my priorities, my brain, and I continued to accept less than I deserved just so I could tell people I had a boyfriend.

At the time of our relationship, I was very insecure. I was struggling with my eating disorder and constantly consumed with thoughts of how I looked. Unfortunately, he also cared deeply about how things appeared to the outside world, including what people thought about me. Some weekends, I would visit him at his college an hour away from my house, only packing a small bag with what I needed to stay the night and for the next morning. On one occasion, in late fall, I knew we would be going out to a party, so I opted just to bring a pair of heeled booties as my shoe of choice. We had a great night, and in the morning, we made plans to eat in the dining hall before I went home. When we got to the dining hall, he looked down at my feet in the only pair of shoes I thought to bring, my booties. "You cannot go in there in those," he stated as he pointed at my feet, obviously annoyed. "Why?" I questioned, thinking nothing of it. "Because it is 9 a.m. and you are wearing heeled shoes. People don't wear that stuff here. You have to wait outside. It is embarrassing. I don't want people to stare and say things." So there I stood in the brisk autumn morning as he went inside to get us food. Standing outside for twenty minutes, alone, on a strange college campus as people walking in and out of the dining hall give you strange looks, now that was embarrassing.

Also, might I add I am in college now, and I wear booties all the time, any time of day, and I get compliments, so thank you very much!

From time to time, I also received unwelcome comments about my body and style: "Did you gain weight? Your boobs grew. That dress doesn't look good on your body. Those shoes make your feet look big. You look slutty in that. Um... that's an interesting choice..." I tried not to show it on my face, but each comment silently dragged me further down the already deep insecurity hole. Here I was, with my boyfriend, who was supposed to love me and find me attractive, but he was pointing out everything he didn't like. Things I didn't even realize were issues until he brought them up!

Regardless of the comment or intention, anyone making unsolicited comments about *your* body is not okay. I never asked for his opinion, nor did I want it. I dress for me. My body is mine, and what I chose to do with my body is my decision. I, unfortunately, didn't have this mentality at the time, so instead of thinking "whatever" to his comments, I let them affect me and fuel my already blistering insecurities.

After a year of being together, a year of some good, and a whole lot of, "Livia, what are you thinking? This is not a healthy relationship," I finally ended things and set myself free.

I always thought I wanted a relationship like I saw in the movies: love letters, surprises, dancing in the rain, rocks thrown at the window, boom boxes held to the sky, singing together in a musical. But what I really want is someone who loves me in sweatpants, with no makeup, and on a bad day. Who is not with me because I am "convenient" or because I make a good accessory. But because we make each other happy and bring out each other's best selves. I want to be with someone who supports me and encourages me. I want someone who does not want to change me. No amount of flowers, romantic gestures, "I love you," or "I am sorry, it won't happen again" should make up for someone treating you badly or making you feel less-than. If someone doesn't make you feel cared for, safe, and happy, they are not the one! Even though I thought I wanted the coveted title of being someone's "girlfriend," the title didn't mean anything because I wasn't happy being *his* girlfriend.

Looking back on the relationship, I now realize a lot of what he said that made me question myself had nothing to do about me and everything to do about him. He was insecure about how he would be perceived. He wasn't okay being alone and needed someone on his arm. He tied his worth to the way he appeared to others. At the end of the day: if someone is not ready to give you love or the love you deserve, it might mean they do not have that love yet for themselves. And that's okay. No one is to blame. It does not mean neither of you is worthy. It just means that inner work needs to be done. As Leo Buscaglia once said, "To love others, you must love yourself... You can only give others what you have yourself."

REALIZING A RELATIONSHIP IS UNHEALTHY

In a Psychology Today article, the author outlines the hallmarks between a positive, healthy relationship and an unhealthy, toxic relationship:

- "Healthy relationships are characterized by:
  - compassion,
  - security,
  - safety,
  - freedom of thinking,
  - sharing, listening,
  - mutual love and caring,
  - healthy debates and disagreements,
  - and respectfulness, especially when there are differences in opinions.
- Toxic relationships are characterized by:
  - insecurity,
  - abuse of power and control,
  - demandingness,
  - selfishness,
  - self-centeredness,

- criticism,

- negativity,

- dishonesty,

- distrust,

- demeaning comments and attitudes,

- and jealousy" (Carter, 2011).

Healthy relationships will leave you feeling happy and energized while unhealthy relationships leave you feeling down, depressed, and depleted.

Unhealthy relationships do not only affect your emotions and leave you feeling insecure, but they also have profound effects on your physical and mental wellbeing. A USC Keck School of Medicine study found that being in bad relationships increases one's risk of developing heart problems (such as a fatal heart attack) than those in healthy relationships. Another USC study found that women in relationships with high levels of conflict are more likely to have high blood sugar levels, high blood pressure, and high rates of obesity (Forbes, 2018). So, if it isn't impacting your mental health, chances are it's impacting your physical health. Or it's impacting both, and you don't realize it.

UNHEALTHY PATTERNS CAN BE PREVALENT IN ALL RELATIONSHIPS YOU HAVE

Unhealthy relationships don't just happen in romantic partnerships but can occur in any relationship you are in. You can have unhealthy relationships with friends, family members, bosses, employees, anyone. I personally have had my fair share of friend relationships that I have had to walk away from.

Friend relationships with people who I once considered a best friend, but as time passed, we changed, grew apart, and in the end, the friendship was bringing me down more than lifting me up. Although it is never fun to have to walk away or leave someone who once was a huge part of your life, in the end, you will both be better off.

We often fear endings, avoid saying goodbye, but at a point, depending on the person and relationship, staying does more harm than good. It is like a first car: the one that you first learned to drive in, the one you used for late-night food runs, the one you drove to school every day, and to your best friend's house every Friday. After a while—and one too many times hitting the curb—the maintenance of that old car is more costly than starting fresh with a new car. It might be scary or sad to let the old one go, the car that took you to so many places, one you spent so much time and energy on, one that is full of memories and history. But at a certain point, you have to let it go. It served its purpose, the memories, energy, time, and effort were not a waste, but as time has gone on, things have changed, shifted, and it no longer works the way it is supposed to. While some things may last forever, other things don't. When you notice that something is not working the way it used to, it might be an indicator that it's time to move on to something new.

SOME REASONS AS TO WHY WE STAY IN BAD RELATIONSHIPS:

1. Standards

According to a study by Edward et al., the single most important factor in determining whether women stay in or leave their relationships is based on relationship satisfaction.

Satisfaction is a subjective experience and is tightly based on what you view as your comparison level or standard. Standards are qualities that a person wants a partner to meet while comparison level is based on what you expect to receive in a relationship. If someone has a low comparison level, they are more likely to stay in a bad relationship for longer; their low expectations are being met as they don't expect many benefits from the relationship (Luciano and Orth, 2017).

While high standards can often feel like our dating pool is very limited, it is important to maintain standards for how you expect to be treated in a relationship.

2. Priorities

In my previous relationships or "things," I have dated the guy's potential rather than their reality. Focusing on their good traits while ignoring the bad. I was once "seeing" this guy for six months where all we did was meet up about once a week and sit in his dorm room and talk. Well... it was more like he talked at me for hours. I would just sit there listening to him talk about debate, his fraternity, anything I could care less about, and then leave two hours later without so much as a goodbye hug. I kept seeing him because he was friendly, ambitious, and had some qualities I was looking for, but I should have ended it months earlier when he called me (after canceling last-minute plans), and for the hour we "talked," my only contribution was the occasional, "Oh wow, that's cool, and uh-huh."

Many of my friends have shared similar experiences, although none can say they talked to a guy for two hours straight about debate. (I have never been in debate, nor have any interest in it.) This is not unusual, though. We often see the good in a relationship and turn a blind eye to the bad. Researchers have investigated this and found that individuals tend to value the positive characteristics their partners display more than other characteristics (Fletcher et al., 2000). For example, if your partner was considerate but not generous over the course of your relationship, you would value thoughtfulness more than generosity (Fugère, 2017). Our priorities change, and we upgrade the importance of positive traits our partners possess and downgrade the importance of negative characteristics.

3. "There are no good fish in the sea"
Backed by research and personal experience, an individual is more likely to leave their relationship if they perceive there is a preferable alternative, but if someone believes there isn't a "better one out there," they are likely to continue staying in the undesirable relationship, even if an alternative is being single (Edwards et al., 2010).

Admittedly, I knew I stayed with "talks too much" boy for way too long, but in my mind, there was no better alternative I knew of. So, I continued to settle on late nights being talked at. Looking back, I would have been much better off alone, but at the time, I viewed being alone as a less desirable alternative.

4. Manipulation
There are many manipulation tactics partners use to make someone stay in a relationship. Emotional manipulation consists of things such as belittling, demeaning, gaslighting, or even threats of violence (Buss and Shackelford, 1997). Emotional manipulation can take the form of using someone's insecurities against them, using fear to control the other person, being passive-aggressive or using the silent treatment, making generalizations such as "you never..." as well as lying

and denying the truth (Villines, 2019). Ultimately, manipulation is used to have power over someone and is used to either benefit themselves in some way or make the other partner feel scared to leave.

5 · Investment

This can be both time investment and shared investments like houses, children, pets. According to a study by Rego et al., if we have invested a lot of time, effort, or resources into a relationship, we are more likely to stay and continue investing in it, even when we might not be happy, or it might not be best for us. As humans, we are loss-averse. We prefer to avoid losses than to acquire an equivalent gain. So, in relationships, we are more likely to continue unhappy situations once we feel we have invested a lot of time, money, and effort.

It does not matter if you are with someone for ten months or ten years, although it is incredibly hard, painful, and will likely be for a while. If you are not happy or safe, it is time for a fresh start.

THERE IS A WAY OUT

If you ever find yourself in an unhealthy relationship, one that leaves you feeling worse about yourself, feels unsafe, drains your energy, leaves you unfulfilled, is marked by drama or angst, any of these, there is a solution.

There is a way out.

The first step is to recognize that you are in one. To admit to yourself or others that this is not healthy and needs addressing.

The second step is to believe you are deserving of better, you should not be treated this way, and that you are deserving of love and compassion. This step does not always come easily. Seeking support from a trusted individual can often help. For me, that was my mom. For you, it could be a friend, a sibling, a school counselor, anyone who makes you feel safe.

The third step is to either work toward fixing the problems if the other is willing or distance yourself from the source of the toxicity. In some circumstances, you can move forward, and things can get better. Other times, it is important to walk away. Even if it is hard, your future self will thank you.

BETTER IS COMING

Many times, people come into our lives for a reason and sometimes only for a season. No matter how long someone is in your life, they are there to teach you something. Let them go when they are supposed to and appreciate the lesson they leave you with. There is always better out there. There are better people, better days, better experiences, better feelings to come. Wait for the better. It will come. The more time you spend alone and learning to love yourself, the more you learn about your values, your deal breakers, and create higher standards for who you bring into your life. The good ones are worth the wait.

PART THREE:

LACKING

CHAPTER 8

GO ALL-IN

—

"The only limit to the height of your achievements is the reach of your dreams and your willingness to work for them."

—MICHELLE OBAMA; FORMER FIRST LADY

It was during PE class in the fifth grade when I first realized I am not meant to be a runner. Each year they had us run a timed mile around the track. Just four laps around a track should be easy, but boy was I wrong. I didn't make it even two laps before nearly passing out. My heart was beating so fast I could hear it in my ears. And to make matters worse, as I stood in the middle of the track gasping for air, the athletic kids were lapping me! I ended up walking off the track and never finishing the mile, making excuses that I had exercise-induced asthma and woke up feeling sick to hide my embarrassment. Everyone finished but me.

That day confirmed three things for me: 1) I hate running. 2) I am not and will never be a runner. 3) I am a damn good actress when it comes to making up excuses.

It was not until I was fourteen years old that I actually ran a full mile, and it was only because I had to for high school soccer tryouts. I didn't make the team. Since when was running a mile in under eight minutes thirty seconds a requirement?

For fourteen blissful years of my life, I avoided the atrocity that is running, and that is mostly thanks to "conveniently" having period craps anytime we had another mile day in PE. And as it turned out, all my friends had cramps at the same time, even those whose period wasn't due anytime soon, or didn't get any periods at all!

But in 2019, September 7th to be exact, I ran 13.1 miles, willingly. I know. I am insane. Between the years of fourteen and twenty, I did not fall in love with running. Yes, I was able to run more than a mile. Yes, I worked out regularly. Yes, I owned a good pair of running shoes. But no, I still hated running. Needless to say, the half marathon was not a fun little hobby of mine. Rather, it was a way to prove to myself that no matter what I want in life, I can achieve it.

The summer before my half marathon, I was starting from scratch. While I was fit from my workouts and obsession with Orangetheory—a group fitness studio focused on total-body, heart rate-based workouts—I couldn't run three miles, let alone a half marathon. I researched and created my own sixteen-week running plan and set out to run three to four times a week and cross-train on nonrunning days. I was in DC for the summer, working at my internship three days a week and as a server the other four. But every day before work, I would train, running the same two to three loops because that was all I knew. Although it was hard to motivate myself, I continued to show up and just start running, one foot in front of the other. My motivation was fueled by my strong "why" behind my actions. Every morning I got up to run, I was doing it for myself, proving that I am stronger, more dedicated, more able than I think. My "why" was to work on myself every day, little by little. My "why" helped get my butt up and out the door. A good post-run breakfast also helped.

Every running morning, my alarm would sound at 6 a.m. as the sun peeked through the blinds. Without a moment's hesitation, I would fling myself out of bed and get ready. The faster I got myself out the door, the less time I would have to convince myself to go back to bed. Once my workout clothes were on, my hair fastened in a ponytail, and shoes laced up, I would make my way to the kitchen to eat my go-to pre-workout snack: a banana with peanut butter. I'd stretch out the time it would take me to eat the snack because I knew as soon as I was done, my earbuds would go in, and it would be go time. I hated go time.

Before each run, I would go up and down the short length of the block to stretch and prime my body for the run. Then, before I had time to process what was about to happen or talk myself out of it, I opened up my run tracking app and hit the start button. My legs would take over as I flung myself down the tree-lined neighborhoods of DC. Even at 6:15 a.m., the summer heat was already making a strong appearance, quickly causing beads of sweat to form a crown around my head. With each stride, my heart pumped faster, and I envisioned my legs growing stronger.

As easy as I made the entire process sound, here's what was actually going through my mind:

"Okay, you are at the beginning. Just take it easy, and you'll make it through."

"This song is so good. I got this."

"Okay, nope. Not this song. It just makes me relive middle school all over again." *shudder*

"Ugh, how much longer do I need to go?"

"Okay, if you pick up your pace, you can make that stop light."

"I just need carbs; lots and lots of carbs after this."

"I have never been so thirsty in my entire life."

"I would do anything for a huge glass of water right now."

"Three more miles left. I want to cry."

"Damn, it's getting so hot, and it's not even 7 a.m. yet."

"Wait, these houses are beautiful."

"I wonder how much someone has to run to like it because I am not sure I ever will."

"Last .5 miles, you got this. You have come so far."

"Yay, you're done. Food time!"

The post-run endorphins and the post-run food kept me going for the day. Because as soon as I showered, ate, and got ready, it was back out the door to go work.

It was a lot, but I was the happiest I have ever been. I was doing this challenge for me, and although the running bug never bit me, the feeling of accomplishment propelled me through.

On the day of my half-marathon, I did not set a goal to achieve a specific time. I just wanted to survive and eat pancakes afterward. Two hours and one minute later, I finished third in my age group for females, twenty to twenty-four years old.

I got a medal, a third-place plaque, and pancakes. It was a great day—mostly because of the pancakes! That day, I proved to myself that no matter what I want in life, with the right mindset and attitude, I could make it happen. It was not the 13.1-mile run I was most proud of. It was my perseverance for the last sixteen weeks.

Over sixteen weeks, I built a reputation with myself. I planned and trained on my own. I didn't have an accountability partner or someone to help get me out the door. It was all me. I built confidence and now know when I say I am going to do something, I will. Even when all I want to do is stop, I will keep pushing. And when things get hard, I just get stronger.

So when I got home, I opened up my notes app and drafted the chapters for my next goal: this book.

MOTIVATION DOES NOT LEAD TO ACTION

Something I've learned first-hand while writing this book is motivation does not lead to action. Rather it is the action that leads to motivation (Bokhari, 2020). Think of it this way: when artists are in a rut with their work, they don't just sit at home and hope that inspiration strikes. They go out and explore. They try new art forms, go to art galleries, and study different artists' works. They act to become inspired and motivated.

And to appeal to my science-folk out there, Newton's first law of motion states: an object will not change its motion unless acted upon. If a body is at rest, it will stay at rest, and if a body is in motion, it will stay in motion. If we wait for motivation to cause action, we are at rest and might be waiting for a long time. But if we use an action to spark motivation, we are creating momentum for ourselves. We are making progress.

When I first started this book, I didn't set a specific time to write. I just waited for inspiration to strike. When that moment came, I would rush to my laptop and let the words flow onto the page. In the first three months, I kept waiting for motivation to come that would allow me to write to my heart's content. But after twelve weeks, I only had a few meager stories.

I began to realize if I wanted to get this book done, I needed to change my method of action. I needed to allocate time to sitting down and writing each week. It didn't matter if what I wrote was good. I just needed to get my thoughts down on paper and worry about making it sound pretty later on. So, I started to dedicate time every day to writing, reading, editing, researching. The agreement I made with myself was that all I had to do was spend at least one hour every day on my book. An hour out of the day is less than 5 percent of the day. I could commit to doing that.

Lo and behold, as soon as I sat down and started typing black letters onto a white page, I'd feel a spark of motivation, and words would rapidly fill the blank space. Sometimes an hour flew by. Sometimes an hour would lead to four. Sometimes an hour led to a whole chapter. Sometimes an hour was painful. Sometimes it took redirecting my focus from social media back to the document every ten minutes.

It didn't matter if I was in the mood to write or not. The action of opening my laptop and lighting a candle (a ritual I created for myself) caused my motivation. All I did was sit down and let my mind take control of my fingers hitting the keys.

Now I want to be clear. This is not about overworking yourself until exhaustion. The goals you make have to be realistic and attainable for you. Just because you set a goal does not mean you need to work yourself into the ground to achieve it. You do not need to always be taking action and working in order to be successful. When I talk about taking action, I mean taking action when it works with your action plan and into your day.

In six months, I finished the first draft of my book.

For the first three months, I relied on my motivation to spark action, and I only wrote six thousand words. In the second three months, my action caused my motivation, and I ended up writing 44,000 words.

In the same amount of time, but with a different method, I was able to be more than seven times more productive.

All you need to do to get started is to start. Don't wait for the perfect moment or until you have everything planned and ready to go. Because the truth is, timing will never be right, and you might never feel completely ready. Just start. Just do something.

THE FIVE-SECOND RULE

Best-selling author Mel Robbins whose TEDxTalk "How to stop screwing yourself over" has over twenty-six million views, came up with "The Five-Second Rule"—a rule for going after your goals. The rule states that when you feel an impulse to act, count to five and then do it without a second thought. In reference to her rule, Mel writes: "If you have an impulse to act on a goal, you must physically move within five seconds, or your brain will kill the idea." Don't wait to second guess yourself, come up with excuses, or put it off for a day. Count to five, then go. As Mel says, "Whatever your goals are, show the world, and yourself, that you're serious by taking action, however insignificant that action may seem, *right now.*"

And once you do something, one thing, the rest comes easy.

All you need is one easy task to cross off and get the ball rolling.

It's something you can do first thing in the morning.

... Any ideas?

In a 2014 commencement speech to the University of Texas at Austin, Naval Admiral William McRaven said: "If you make your bed every morning, you will have accomplished the first task of the day. It will give you a small sense of pride, and it will encourage you to do another task and another and another. By the end of the day, that one task completed will have turned into many tasks completed. Making your bed will also reinforce the fact that little things in life matter."

Moral of the story: go make your bed.

GOAL SETTING

In college, I was a Peer Health Partner (PHP). As a PHP, I had the unglamorous role of teaching a health class to a group of twenty first-year students. Twenty students who did not want to sit in a small dark room and listen to someone two years older than them talk about nutrition and good sleep patterns. Twenty students who looked at me like a deer in headlights when I asked them a question. Good thing they weren't getting graded on participation because I am pretty sure awkward silences do not count. Let's just say class finished rather quickly, and I let them out fifteen minutes early every time, and for that reason, they loved me.

In class, we covered a wide array of topics, one of which was goal setting. During the goal-setting class, I had students create goals for themselves using the SMART goal framework. SMART goals stand for: Specific, Measurable, Achievable, Realistic, Time-bound goals. By following the SMART goal structure, students were more likely to achieve their desired outcome.

A study by psychology professor Dr. Gail Matthews proves the efficacy of SMART goals. In her study, Dr. Matthews recruited a diverse group of 267 individuals and had them identify their top goals. The participants were asked to rate their goals according to difficulty, significance, and the extent to which they have the ability to accomplish them. After participants had chosen a goal, they were divided into five groups. Group one was instructed not to write down their goal. They just had to think about it. Groups two through five wrote their goals down. Groups three, four, and five also wrote down an action plan. Groups four and five gave their goal and action commitment to a friend. And group five was directed to report weekly updates on their progress.

The results of the study showed that participants in the fifth group were 76 percent successful at accomplishing their goals (Tabaka, 2019). This is 33 percent higher than group one, where there was a 43 percent success rate.

Participants were able to increase the likelihood of achieving their goals when they wrote them down, created a clear action plan, and enlisted a support system to keep them accountable.

Think of it like my writing this book. If one day I just decided to write a book and began typing, I'd probably hit many roadblocks. My book would not have a clear direction, and the chapters would be messy. I probably would give up before I truly got started.

In reality, when I decided my next goal was to write a book, I started by creating an action plan and defining a clear vision. Before writing, I made sure to plan the theme, title, chapters, and stories. I also knew I needed some help, so I joined an author program that kept me accountable and guided me through each step. This was a slightly different approach from when I ran my half-marathon. When I started marathon training, I wanted to test my abilities and do it all myself. I did not want an accountability partner. However, when starting my book, I knew I needed and wanted additional support, so I found it. Your goals and processes to reach those goals should be tailored specifically to your needs. The way you approach one goal may be completely different from how you do a second goal. But in both cases, I had a clear goal in mind, a plan of action, and deadlines with checkpoints.

Writing a book seemed daunting at the beginning, but by having a clear timeframe and mini-goals throughout, it made the process manageable and enjoyable!

By following the SMART goal structure, I was able to have my book published ten months after I began writing on top of being a full-time college student.

SMART GOAL STRUCTURE:

- **Specific:** Are your goals clear and well-defined?
  - Example: I want to run the Craft Classic half marathon on September 7th, 2019, in Atlanta, GA.
  - The narrower your goal and the clearer you are, the easier it will be to tailor your plan, measure progress, and create a realistic timeline.

- **Measurable:** Do you have a way to measure and assess progress as you go? Create smaller goals and check points to get you on the right track.

  o Example: Creating a running plan that assigns a certain distance to run every day and sets rest days. Having the running plan gradually increase the distance to get you acclimated to running long distances.

  o Create small goals and check points by cutting down your goal in halves. For instance, if your goal is to buy a million-dollar house in five years, cut that goal in half, so at 2.5 years, you would need to have saved $500,000. Then cut it in half again. At 1.25 years, you would need to save $250,000. Another half, at nine months, that's $125,000. At three months, you need $62,500 and six weeks, $31,250. By creating checkpoints with mini-goals throughout, it makes sure you're on the right track.

- **Achievable:** Can the goal be completed in the time allotted?

  o Example: Deciding to run a half marathon a day before with no training would make it very hard and painful to complete.

  o Using the measurable check points, work backgrounds to see if your goal makes sense in the time allotted. Could you realistically save $31,250 in six weeks? Or would this take a year? Maybe instead of five years to buy a million-dollar house, a ten or twenty-year goal would make more sense. Using your current circumstances, abilities, environment, financial, mental, emotional, and physical health, is this time frame realistic?

- **Realistic:** Does this goal make sense for you? Is it relevant to your life purpose?
  - Example: Running a half marathon was relevant to me because I had a strong "why" behind it. I wanted to prove I can do hard things.
  - When creating goals, dive deep into your motivation behind them. Do you want to do this goal for you, or is it for external validation? Is this goal applicable to the larger vision for your life, or is there another goal that could be more effective? You will be more committed to achieving your goal if you have a strong motivation behind your why.

- **Time-bound:** Do you have a specific time frame for when you want to complete the goal?
  - Example: September 7th, 2019
  - By having an end date, it creates urgency and puts necessary pressure on getting things moving and happening.

Start now! Start working on those goals you have been pushing aside because the time isn't "right." You will never be younger than you are today. It's time to start working toward what you want. It's time to make your bed and get to work.

Ready:

one
two
three
four
five

CHAPTER 9

IT'S OKAY NOT TO BE OKAY

———

"Difficult times can define us, they can diminish us, or they can develop us, you decide."

—JIM KWIK; RENOWNED BRAIN COACH

Sad, irritated, anxious, happy, stuck. I am not okay.
In fact, this whole year, I haven't been, and I have oscillated between a range of five emotions. It's 2020; need I say more?

The new decade started with anticipation and excitement for what many believed would be an incredible year, including myself. This was supposed to be the year of celebrations, graduations, and marriages. The year people started exciting new chapters by going to college, moving to a new city, or starting a new job. This was supposed to be a great year.

This was supposed to be my year.

It was the year I would study abroad in London with my best friends. The year I would get my dream job as an event planner in DC. The year I would embark on my last year of college. The year I would live out my detailed life plan that had been on track up until March 13th, 2020. Instead of the year many were expecting, 2020 became the year of loss as we sheltered in our homes and distanced ourselves from the ones we love.

Everything changed in an instant: sweatpants became the new go-to attire, home became the new office, our screens became our source of connection, and masks became the new love language.

Smiles hid behind masks, and distance was put in between strangers, friends, loved ones. Groceries scrubbed; hugs forgotten.

Lives were lost, relationships tested, and pivotal life moments were put on hold or streamed through a computer. For over a year, we lived with uncertainty, loss, fear, and bouts of hope.

I did not lose someone close to me this year. I am so incredibly thankful for my family's and my health. I want to offer my sincere condolences to anyone who is grieving. Whatever you are going through, whether it be loss of life, loss of a relationship, loss of time, loss of plans, your feelings are valid.

As each plan I had crumbled, my anxiety took me hostage. I lost my job, my relationship, my senior year of college, and myself. I mentally reverted back to the place I was in 2016, depressed.

Instead of spending the summer with a clipboard in hand, making sure gorgeous venues were decorated to perfection with stunning floral arrangements and billowy linens, I spent the summer in leggings on my couch binge-watching *Love Island*, a British reality TV show. I spent every day in bed, unable to do anything other than a workout for an hour—only because I was in the habit of working out. The way I coped with the uncertainty and sadness was through isolating myself.

I resisted talking about my feelings. I resisted talking about pretty much anything. I was so entangled in my negative emotions that my parents would ask me how my day was, and I would snap at them and break down in tears. This happened at least once a week. They wanted to help. They pushed for me to open up to them because I was clearly not okay. I wouldn't let them in. I wanted to be alone and to deal with my feelings, alone. For over ten months, I pushed people I loved away. I pushed them away because I thought I could handle my emotions on my own. I thought I could be my own therapist and just "figure it out." It turns out I make a bad self-therapist.

LEARNING FROM THE LOW

I reached a point that I became so tired of living the way I was. I was tired of feeling sorry for the situation, tired of being grumpy and sad, tired of being alone, tired of wasting time away. I knew who I wanted to be, I knew what I wanted to do with my life, but I was living as the opposite of that vision.

I didn't like the way I felt. I didn't enjoy spending hours upon hours in bed, watching shows, and endlessly scrolling through social media. Sure, it is fine and fun to do sometimes, but doing that every day just made me feel lost and detached. All day, I stewed in my negative emotions, not making an effort to do anything differently. And because I didn't make an effort to change, I continued to feel stuck for months.

I've read enough self-development books to have a plethora of quotes like Jack Canfield's "There is only one person responsible for the quality of your life. That person is you." drilled into my head. I knew I couldn't keep isolating myself and living in a depressed state. I knew it would take time and energy, but if anything was going to change, it was up to me. So, I used the vision I have of who I want to be and where I want to go as fuel to push past the mental pain—as Dr. Michael Beckwith says, "Pain pushes until the vision pulls."

Regardless of if I was in a happy state or sad state, I was expending a lot of energy, and I no longer wanted to spend the energy on my pity party.

When I finally had enough and realized if I wanted to feel better, it was up to me. I made a change and worked to get unstuck.

The first thing I did was change up my scenery.

I stopped spending all day isolated in my room and made an effort to connect with others. I spent the rest of my days downstairs or outside, either connecting to nature or just being around people I love. The small change of moving my space helped break the monotony of my previous days. The change of place allowed me to start establishing new habits, developing healthier coping mechanisms, and partaking in activities that engage and energize me.

I started leaving my phone upstairs, physically distancing myself from a source that drains my energy and leaves me feeling bleh. I replaced the hours I spent binge-watching Netflix, with reading, drafting chapters of this book, or any other positive activity. I allowed myself to watch TV and scroll on my phone at night, but I made sure to spend my days engaged in things that left me feeling good.

With all the extra time I had left, I reflected and took inventory of my life. What had I done that made me proud? Who and what brought me joy? Which behaviors and habits of mine were dysfunctional? What was I grateful for? What thought pattern did I need to let go of? What could I learn from the lows I experienced? It turns out a lot!

- I started becoming flexible, which was a skill I had been working on for years. This was not the year for plans, and I had to adapt to not living five steps in the future.

- I started practicing gratitude which helped me to stop, sit with the moment, and take in my surroundings. Being grateful and thinking of the things I appreciate in my life allowed me to live more in the moment and experience each day with open arms and no expectations.

- I learned material items really do not bring as much happiness as experiences do. Unfortunately, I learned this after spending way too much money on retail therapy. The little experiences that I had, even just picking up my favorite takeout and enjoying it at home, left me with a greater, longer-lasting feeling of joy than ripping open a new package.

- I realized I couldn't do it all, I needed help, and when I talked about my feelings with loved ones, it was easier to process my emotions. A good cry can do wonders.

- I finally stopped and reflected on how far I had come and how much I had accomplished. For so many years, I kept pushing myself to be more, be smarter, be prettier, be better, but I never took the time to appreciate my wins and how far I had come in my development.

- The biggest lesson I took away was how precious and short life is. In a day, things dramatically changed, and the world shut down. Things we took for granted, like a handshake with a stranger or going into the office, were suddenly taken from us. We started missing the small awkward conversations with acquaintances and our old routines. Heck, I even miss spending all day studying in the library. I realized I did not fully appreciate my life and the people in it. Only until things were gone did I realize how special and important they were. This year taught me to never miss an opportunity to tell someone I love them or miss them. It reminded me to spend as much time as I can with people I care about and doing things I enjoy. Going forward, I'll cherish every moment as much as I can.

These lessons will keep having to be learned. I have in no way mastered any of these. But through reflection, realization, and *a lot* of self-awareness, I was able to grow and release some negative patterns. Little by little, I was able to gain a clearer outlook.

I don't believe I would have learned these lessons (or at least as soon) had the events of 2020 not taken place. If everything continued going as planned, I would have continued living each day for the next, not taking time to slow down and appreciate my life, being too self-focused to see those around me, always rushing to accomplish the next task.

As Eckhart Tolle wrote in his book, *The Power of Now*, "Growth is usually considered positive, but nothing can grow forever. If growth, of whatever kind, were to go on and on, it would eventually become monstrous and destructive. Dissolution is needed for new growth to happen. One cannot exist without the other."

Often, your darkest hours and worst days are the ones you gain the most from. The hard times give you incredible insights into what is and isn't working. It sheds light on dysfunctional thoughts or people in your life. It shows you that the path you are currently on might not be for you. It offers you a fresh perspective to objectively look at where you came from, where you are, and where you are going.

GROWING FROM THE PAIN

If you haven't taken a spin class before, you might not know amidst the sweating, dark room, and loud music, the instructors offer some wisdom from their lives or Pinterest boards. While a lot of the "wisdom" are statements such as: "If you can get through this ride, you can get through anything" or "The way you ride this bike is the way you live your life." Sometimes the instructors make a comment that resonates deeply with me. One of these times was in the early stages of the pandemic in a virtual spin class.

My spin instructor stared at the camera through my computer screen as my resistance on my bike made it feel like I was biking vertically up Mount Everest. I listened intently to her story to distract me from the burning sensation taking over my legs. She started recounting a time she was riding in an Uber through downtown Boston. The area they were passing through was under construction. A plan in store for massive skyscrapers to grace the city skyline—although, at the time, there were just huge pits in the ground. Her Uber driver pointed out that in order to build a skyscraper that would shine above the other buildings, standing tall in the sky for all to see, you have to dig to the lowest point in the ground. Before building occurs, workers dig and dig to reach rock-bottom.

Once they have dug to a low enough point, they can begin to build upward, one floor at a time. Each floor, creating a stronger foundation, grounding the building so it can withstand all that height and any weather condition. The taller the skyscraper, the more stable it needs to be, the lower you have to dig.

You and I, we are just like those skyscrapers. In order to reach new heights, be seen and admired, provide comfort to others, to avoid rattling and breaking in extreme weather, you have to be rooted firmly in the ground. In order to reach your peak, you have to experience a low and build gradually, one step at a time. The lows we experience make us grounded. They teach us important life lessons we might not have learned or fully appreciated had we not faced a rough patch. They reveal hidden truths about our lives, circumstances, and intended destinations. If you are open to see it, there is a meaning and valuable lesson in every experience. Even an Uber ride can offer profound wisdom.

In whatever hard place you are in, give yourself grace and compassion and know that the times when growth really starts to happen are when we hit a low point. At your lowest moments, think to yourself, "I may be in a low right now, but that is only because I am getting ready for growth to happen." This low moment is setting the foundation for you to be grounded in who you are, what you want, and rise high.

But you cannot rush healing. Sometimes low points last for a long time, and that is okay. It's important not just to shove those feelings down and pretend to be happy so you can start "going up" again. In order to work through our feelings, we need to really process our negative emotions and feel what we need to feel. Take your time, and go at your own pace. There is no timeline for growth.

What has helped me in my low moments is to step back and remember all the times I have felt down. All the times I didn't think something would change, or I would get to a better state, but then I did. No feeling will last forever. You won't be happy every day, but you also won't be sad every day. There are many days I have woken up in a down mood, all day feeling fatigued, sad, and not myself. But somehow, the next day, I am back to my happy self again.

In the low moments, just continuously telling myself "this too shall pass" helps me feel lighter and release some of the emotional pain I am experiencing.

Another way that helps me move out of a low is by reminding myself I am ultimately in control of the way I speak to myself and the actions I take. At any moment, I could make a change to shift my energy. Just building up the energy to go for a walk outside or read my favorite book will help shift my mood. It does not always take much. Wanting to feel better and getting yourself immersed in something outside of yourself, whether it be going in nature, reading a book, baking, doing something for someone else, or exercising, can do wonders.

The next time you are in a low, stuck, icky place, know that no matter how big or heavy yours feels, no matter how significant or insignificant it may seem, you are allowed to feel how you feel. But, at the end of the day, it is up to you to bring yourself out of that feeling and into a better place.

HARD TIMES MAKE US WHO WE ARE

I am sure we all know and adore Oprah Winfrey. How could you not? That woman is walking wisdom and love. But Oprah didn't get to where she is today as an American talk show host, television producer, actress, author, and philanthropist the easy way. Oprah has overcome great adversity in her life. She was born into poverty in the rural south during the Civil Rights Movement and was looked after by her abusive grandmother as her mother worked as a maid. Oprah was also molested many times as a child and fled home at thirteen after years of abuse. At fourteen, she became pregnant. Her son was born prematurely and died soon after he was born.

In high school, Oprah was sent to Nashville to live with her dad, where she landed a job doing radio. Her radio gig eventually led to a position on the local evening news in Chicago when she was nineteen ("Oprah Winfrey," 2021). From there, her career slowly but surely took off as she moved to different radio stations, took on roles in movies, interviewed celebrities, coauthored books, and launched her own production company. Each step of the way bringing her to where she is today: a household name and one of the most influential women in the world. Despite her difficult and traumatic beginnings, Oprah was able to rise above and open doors for herself. She used her background to provide comfort and encouraging advice to help others overcome their own obstacles. Through all of the hardships she faced, she saw more for herself. She channeled her past into making her stronger, into realizing her purpose in life is to be a benefactor.

Motivational coach Tony Robbins grew up with an alcoholic mother who frequently used drugs and was abusive toward Robbins and his two siblings. In an interview later in life, Robbins describes part of the reason for his success is because "I had to protect my brother and sister [from the abuse], so I became a practical psychologist just out of necessity." At seventeen, Robbins left his chaotic and abusive home life and worked as a janitor and part-time mover to make ends meet. During a moving shift, Robbins started talking to a landlord on site where he first learned about Jim Rohn, a motivational speaker. Rohn's philosophy circled around the belief that "True happiness is not contained in what you get. Happiness is gained by what you become." This sparked something in Robbins, and after saving up for a week and attending a seminar, he approached Rohn and eventually became his protégé. Robbins used his experience working with Rohn to create his own motivational speaking program with his signature high energy personalized approach. By twenty-six, Robbins had become a millionaire, conducted countless seminars, and wrote a best-selling book (Feloni, 2017).

Both individuals offer brilliant wisdom and inspiration to millions of people globally. Both individuals have faced hardships and trauma and have reached a low that is unfathomable to many of us. Both were able to change the narrative and use their rock bottom as a gift. They have built a strong foundation for who they are and what they want to create in the world. They were able to slowly grow and become the extraordinary people they are today because of where they came from. They were able to build their skyscrapers to incredible heights and provide a shelter for all of us—a safe space to go to for guidance. Who knows where they would be today had they not faced their darkest days and grew from there.

Those are obviously two extreme examples of people who faced incredibly difficult experiences and rose to the top. In order to be successful, you do not need to go through early adversity or face trauma. But in life, we all go through our fair share of challenges. In the moment, and maybe for months or years to come, they might be hard and difficult to face head-on. But ultimately, these experiences help shape us and the path we go down. They help us grow, become more self-aware, develop a new perspective, and learn things that might have taken us years to learn. The quote at the beginning of this chapter describes this perfectly. In any hardship you face, you can be defined by it—let it control you and bring you down—or you can let it develop you—let it teach you something and bring you someplace new. In the face of adversity, you get to decide how it will eventually affect you.

My dear friend Grace is the perfect example. Throughout Grace's life, she has been diagnosed with different health issues. Grace has not let her diagnoses get the best of her. Instead, she has used them to fuel her desire to work as a physical therapist, wanting to help men and women through their own health complications. Grace's health diagnoses have also given her a superpower—the superpower of empathy. Grace is the most empathetic person I know, and while she sometimes says, "It's a blessing and a curse," it is one of the reasons Grace is an amazing friend and will be an incredible PT. Instead of being defined or diminished by her hardships, Grace decided they would make her stronger.

It might seem counterintuitive but thank the hard times. Thank the moments you feel like you are going in the wrong direction. Thank the sad moments and the stuck-icky feelings. Each knock down is only setting you up to grow taller and stronger. Each knock down is a gift, teaching you an important lesson or pointing you in a new direction.

BEING OKAY, NOT BEING OKAY

The next time you are feeling low, try using one or some of the following to bring yourself to a better place.

Release

- Can you let go of this? That question is something my mom recently asked me when I was not in the best place. A lot of times, we hold onto emotions and negative thoughts longer than we need to. In fact, according to neuroscientist Jill Bolte Taylor, the lifespan of an emotion is only ninety seconds. In her book, My Stroke of Insight: A Brain Scientist's Personal Journey, Dr. Jill writes, "When a person has a reaction to something in their environment, there's a ninety-second chemical process that happens in the body. After that, any remaining emotional response is just the person choosing to stay in that emotional loop." Long-lasting emotions are with us because we have assigned meaning to them. A feeling of disappointment after not performing well on an exam or at work could last only ninety seconds. But because we give it meaning and attach our thoughts to it, our expectations about how well we should have done, our feelings about our own intelligence, we end up holding onto the negative feeling for much longer.

- As Tony Robbins says, "Nothing in life has any meaning except the meaning we give it." The next time you feel any negative emotion, just sit and observe the emotion rather than getting wrapped up in it or assigning meaning and negative thoughts. Instead of spending all day consumed by the emotion, it will likely last only ninety seconds, and then you can move onto more productive stuff.

Cope

- Healthy coping mechanisms help to change someone's perspective while simultaneously bringing joy and reducing stressful and negative emotions.

- Healthy coping mechanisms look like:
    - Meditating
    - Journaling and reading
    - Stretching and moving your body
    - Talking with a friend
    - Going on a walk
    - Playing music, doing art, creating something
    - Asking for help
    - Enjoying nature

- Choose a few coping mechanisms that you want to start partaking in whenever you are in a low. My personal favorites are going on a walk, working out, or reading.

Connect

- When I am not in a good place, I tend to go inward, isolating myself from everyone as a protection mechanism. However, the time I need social interaction the most is when I am not my best and feel inclined to isolate myself. On many occasions when I have been down, my mom has lovingly forced me to attend an event, see a friend, or hang out with family. Although I have fought back, tried to cancel last minute, or decline the offer, every time I have gone, I have immediately felt better. When I isolate myself, it is just me and my thoughts that can turn into a spiral of negativity and being down on myself. When I make an effort to be social (or forced to be), I am distracted by conversations and can get out of my own head for a while. This could be different for you. If socializing doesn't help you feel better, try spending time connecting to yourself or with nature!

- Another way to get out of a negative thought loop is by doing something for someone else. Kindness releases serotonin which is our feel-good hormone and is responsible for well-being and satisfaction (Providence, 2021). Helping others also helps reduce anxiety and depression, lower stress, boost energy and ease pain. We feel good when we help others, leaving us both better off. A win all around!

As Jen Sincero wrote in her best-selling book, *You Are a Badass*, "Obstacles and challenges are the agents of growth." Without not being okay, or facing hard times, we wouldn't be where we are today. We wouldn't be able to love ourselves at any stage or be confident enough to fight for what is right and what we want. We wouldn't know how strong we truly are and how much we can handle. In order to grow, we need to be knocked down. Hard times show us our resilience. It shows us what matters in life and what is most important to us.

CHAPTER 10

PASSIONS ARE PRIORITIES

———

"Twenty years from now, you will be more disappointed by the things that you didn't do than by the ones you did do."

—MARK TWAIN; WRITER

So far, at age twenty-two, I have had five big passions. Five different things that gave me energy, made me excited, and became a part of my purpose. Five things I have loved to do, whether I was good or not. Five things that got me out of bed in the morning. Five things that have changed who I am becoming and have brought me closer to who I am.

I know I will not just have five passions. I know that throughout different periods of life, I will discover new activities, jobs, experiences, classes that make my heart happy. When I find those things, just like with the other five, I will follow my heart and say "yes."

THE FIRST PASSION: AGE THREE PLUS

When I was little, I loved to perform and put on shows for anyone who would watch. I'd make up elaborate stories, act out a short play, or perform a dance. Singing, however, was out of the question from an early age. You can't win 'em all.

Most evenings, either before or after dinner, I would call my parents and grandparents down to our basement, where we had a little wooden stage tucked in the corner. I'd instruct them to sit on the white pull-out chairs while I took my place, front and center. Although the setting and lighting was far from that in a theatre—there were no spotlights that would follow me and my moves—I made do with the little resources I had. I'd put on a flashlight in the front that acted as a spotlight, making me feel nothing short of a real star. Every night was a different show, and luckily for them, the performances never lasted long before I went off in my own little world, lost in my imagination.

In the summers, my family held a talent show, which, in my eight-year-old mind, was the biggest event of the year. Every year, for the eight years we did it, my cousin, Felisa, and I would perform a dance. A dance we would spend most of the summer choreographing, refining, and practicing until it was an award-winning performance. In the afternoons, as all the cousins played in the lake, perfecting their underwater handstands and jumping off the dock into the cold but comforting water, Felisa and I would secretly escape to go rehearse. I was competitive from a young age, and I wanted to win it (even if we only gave out winners one year, which did not go over well). After months of excitement, weeks of practicing, the day of the talent show would arrive. It was like Christmas part two for me. When dinner finished, everyone made their way to the designated "talent show room." It was a parlor furnished with antique couches, rugs, and chairs. While the audience was forming and ready to watch the new generation of aspiring stars, all the cousins would go upstairs to get performance ready. Which in Felisa's and my case meant matching outfits we had bought the week before, a collection of pieces from the Dollar Store, Goodwill, and Target.

As soon as I took the "stage," the familiar mix of nerves and excitement would flutter through my body. Being in front of a crowd, no matter how big or small, gave me energy. It made me feel unstoppable.

THE SECOND PASSION: AGE FIVE PLUS

Since I was five, I have loved a good party. Not just because a lot of parties have cake—which we have established by now that I love—but because of the energy, the joy, the love, and, well yeah, the yummy food.

From the age of five, I was already in love with event planning. My birthdays were my favorite day of the year. The fact that I was the center of attention was already a huge reason why, but also because I got to plan, come up with creative ideas, pick out decorations, choose the menu, and see all my favorite people. My favorite part was picking out the goodie bag gifts at the Dollar Store.

I was also obsessed with weddings from an early age. As a five-year-old, my dream in life and all I wanted was to be a flower girl. Unfortunately, I never managed to fulfill that dream, but for Christmas that year, my parents bought me a flower girl dress. A dress that I promptly put on and paraded around my house for hours in. Holding a basket of fake flowers to complete the look.

I never felt more magical.

To this day, my love and passion for event planning have not waned. If anything, it has gotten bigger, and I know one day, no matter how long it takes, I will become an event planner.

Sometimes obstacles can get in the way of your passions, and life seems like it's going in a different direction. Maybe your academic major and your passion don't align, a global pandemic happens, and many industries shut down, or something happens in your life that makes it hard to pursue your passion. But if the cause, career, or interest is something you're truly passionate about, you'll keep finding your way back to it.

THE THIRD PASSION: AGE SEVENTEEN PLUS

In high school, my mom and I went to the same gym which had a list of workout classes, one of which was spin class. On one of our frequent mother-daughter walks, she asked if I wanted to try the class with her. When she first suggested it, I thought she was talking about a dance class that involved spinning. My mind jumped to line dancing with cowboy boots before it jumped to a stationary bike. Reluctantly, I agreed to go with her. What started as our Sunday morning tradition, followed by a yummy homemade brunch, turned into a biweekly thing for me. The more I did it, the more excited I was for the next class. I outgrew our gym's spin class schedule and found a boutique spin studio nearby. I was attending classes as many days as my legs could handle. It became a form of therapy for me: forty-five minutes in a dark room, loud music, clublike lights, sweating, dancing, and moving with no judgment from others. I loved every second, even when my lungs were heavy, breathing was hard, and my eyes were blurry with sweat.

Thankfully, when I went off to college, I didn't have to give up spinning. My college offered student-led classes, which I attended twice a week, sometimes being the only person with the instructor. By sophomore year, I was a spin instructor. Every Monday and Wednesday, I looked forward to teaching. It was one of the highlights of my college experience.

To this day, I take spin classes multiple times a week, and a goal of mine is to teach at a spin studio while working a full-time job. That one "yes" to taking the class with my mom, even though I truthfully did not want to, led to my favorite way of exercising and something that has helped both my mind and body.

THE FOURTH PASSION: AGE EIGHTEEN PLUS

When I was eighteen, I bought my first nutrition book. I was in Barnes & Noble one day and saw the book on the bestsellers table. It was during the tail end of my struggle with my eating disorder, and I wanted to learn more about the power food has on the body. So, I bought the book on a whim. Before I knew it, I had a collection of nutrition books stacked on my bedside table. On the weekends, I would sprawl out on our living room couch, the sun beaming through the window, a pink highlighter in hand as I read the dense research-heavy books, strangely engrossed. I even had a dedicated navy-blue spiral-bound notebook for my reading notes. Keeping colorful notes of the information I was reading, just for pleasure.

For a good year, every time I went to a bookstore, I gravitated toward the diet book aisle. While other customers in the aisle were looking to lose weight or heal a physical alignment through food, I was just fascinated by the study of nutrition. I could have spent hours in those stores, skimming through a mountain of books, absorbing as much information as possible, learning more and more. I never came home empty-handed.

As my book collection grew, more notebook pages filled, and my pink sharpie ran out of ink, my passion for nutrition emerged. I became the nutrition expert of the family, with family members coming to me with all their questions and health concerns. When I went to college, I had a full spreadsheet with classes I would need to take to get into nutrition school, and until sophomore year, I took multiple nutrition classes. That dream eventually ended, but even to this day, I have a strong passion for health and fitness, all because I read a book.

Oftentimes, our productive passions arise out of necessity and healing.

Many individuals who were once overweight and started a health journey found a passion for fitness and nutrition, eventually running marathons or starting fitness businesses. Individuals who were once addicts have used their recovery to help others in many different forms. And often those who pursue a career in healthcare have personally dealt with health issues or someone close to them was saved by doctors.

You never know where your journey will take you and what new passions you will discover.

THE FIFTH PASSION: AGE TWENTY-TWO

Growing up, I truthfully loathed English class. I was always much more into math, something with concrete answers and patterns. The ability to write anything and have prompts open to interpretation made me anxious. I liked to be told what to do and to follow an equation. I took as few English classes as I could, which meant I got away with only taking one in college. When I decided to write this book, it was because I had a desire to share some (hopefully) helpful advice, a desire to make someone feel less alone, a desire to write from the perspective of a young adult dealing with insecurities, rejection, and fear. It was not because I grew up wanting to be a writer or because I thought I was a good writer. I thought that it would be a hard challenge, that I would learn how to write better, learn to actually use punctuation properly, and become more self-aware.

What I never intended was to fall in love with writing. On countless occasions, I found myself opening up a document, and before I knew it, I would look at the clock, and hours would have passed. Hours felt like minutes. Writing put me in a state of flow. A state of total immersion in the activity at hand. A state of mind where, as positive psychologist Mihály Csíkszentmihályi described in a *Wired Magazine* interview, "The ego falls away. Time flies. Every action, movement, and thought follows inevitably from the previous one, like playing jazz. Your whole being is involved, and you're using your skills to the utmost." When you are in flow, the mind and body zone into one thing, distractions are gone, time ticks by without notice, and senses become heightened (Cherry, 2021).

I never experienced flow writing a paper for English class, but I did experience flow writing many chapters in this book.

Even when I hit roadblocks and chapters did not come out the way I wanted, I loved the process of writing, and I discovered a new passion of mine.

Just because you hadn't had a good experience with an activity when it was a requirement and rules and guidelines were involved, it doesn't mean you will have the same experience without those boundaries. Maybe you hated art class growing up because of the rigid rules you had to follow, but now you might fall in love with art and the ability to be creative and express yourself in whatever way you want. You could have a passion for dance, but growing up, you didn't like dance because it wasn't the right style for you. Keep trying new things, even things you once thought you "hated." You might have interests, abilities, and talents that you haven't fully discovered.

My passions came from starting. From doing and trying new things. From just saying "yes." I never started something new with an intention to be the best or to make it a career. I went in open-minded and without pressure.

If you have ever thought, "Well, I don't know what I am passionate about," I am here to tell you that you do know. There is something in your life you love, enjoy doing, and brings you energy, but for whatever reason, you have been pushing it aside. Maybe it is because you believe your passion won't make money, or you're too busy or afraid of what others will think. It's hard to prioritize creativity in a world that's constantly telling you to "hustle." Your perception and priorities can easily get clouded by thoughts of what society wants you to do. However, it's only in your hands to change that.

If you enjoy something, do it.

Your passion doesn't need to make you money, it doesn't need to be something you are good at, it doesn't need to "sound cool," and it doesn't need to be your full-time job. All it needs to do is give you energy to be worth it.

Make the time to engage with it. Time is not the issue; the issue is priorities.

Pursuing a passion in whatever way works in your life makes you feel good. In a 2015 study published in The Annals of Behavioral Medicine, researchers found that participants who actively engaged with a hobby they were passionate about were 34 percent less stressed and 18 less sad during the activity and for a while after (Schumer, 2018). Our lives are more enriched when we are engaged with things we want and like to do. And as a result, we become happier and more connected.

So go to those dance classes, to those pottery classes. Keep playing the ukulele and singing. Keep drawing and tie-dying and baking and coding. Just do what you enjoy without putting pressure on yourself.

START BEFORE YOU ARE READY

Entrepreneur and best-selling author Marie Forleo always loved to dance. Specifically hip-hop dance. But while many girls start taking dance lessons when they are young, Marie never did. Despite not having formal teaching, she still loved to dance and was even quite good at it!

As a guest on Ed Mylett's podcast, *The Mylett Show*, Marie detailed her love for dance, stating, "When I was twenty-five, I finally gave myself permission to go take my first official dance class." These classes were at her local NYC Crunch fitness studio, which was all she could afford at the time. Marie kept attending the classes, and not before long, was recognized by an instructor for her good moves. The instructor asked Marie to be a substitute hip-hop dance teacher, to which Marie said "yes" even though she had no idea what she was doing.

In the podcast, she explained how after one of the first dance classes she taught by herself, she was approached by a woman who worked for MTV. The woman complimented Marie's dancing and handed her a business card for her boss who was looking for a choreographer/producer. Marie's first thought jumped to "I am not ready for this. Why couldn't this opportunity come two, or three, or four years later when I know what the heck I am doing, or I am better prepared, or I could actually show up and maybe even land this gig?" However, she realized that this might be the only chance she would have. All she had to do was show up and try. So she did. Marie went to the gig, tried her best, and ended up landing it.

Although she often felt embarrassed because she had no formal training, did not know the dance terminology, and was working with people with years of experience, she didn't give up. While simultaneously bartending and working on her newsletter that eventually grew into her coaching business, Marie kept working harder to become a better dancer, teacher, and choreographer. Because of her effort and making dance a priority, her learning and growth curve was exponential. Before she knew it, her choreographing gig led to her being one of the first Nike dance athletes, starring in fitness videos and choreographing commercials for Nike and Rebok. She told Ed, "That would have never happened if I did not start before I was ready."

Had Marie said "no" at any point, she would likely not be where she is today as a highly successful business owner, author, dancer, host, and entrepreneur. She didn't let her lack of dance experience stop her from taking a dance class. She said "yes" to being a dance teacher, despite having no dance background or professional training. She still auditioned for the MTV position even though she believed she would not get the job. And when she got the job, she accepted because she loved to dance and did not care that pursuing a career in choreography is not the most lucrative career. Marie made her passions a priority.

Let Marie's story motivate you to just try. Don't think, "I can't do that, I won't make money doing that!" Because you don't know for sure. Even if it doesn't bring you the career, the money, the connections, it might bring you fulfillment and happiness, and that's worth a lot in and of itself.

Marie wanted to dance, so she did. She didn't analyze. She didn't think she would make this her career. She didn't shy away from just trying. And you know what, she tried, she had fun, she kept going back, and one thing led to another, and it brought her a career. All Marie did was decide to do something she liked.

What is one thing you can start adding into your daily, weekly, monthly calendar that you have always wanted to try?

YOU NEVER KNOW WHERE THINGS CAN GO

YouTuber, cohost of the *Gals on the Go* podcast, and content creator Brooke Miccio found her passion for content creation through her hobby of making music videos when she was eleven. I have been a follower of Brooke for a few years, and I am grateful to have had the opportunity to interview her about how she found her passion and turned it into a career.

Brooke heard about YouTube when she was in elementary school. At the time, YouTube trends centered around music videos, comedy sketches, and parodies. Brooke enjoyed watching these videos and decided she wanted to make her own, so in 2010, Brooke started her own channel. "I found this community of people my own age making little skits or music videos. So, I recruited all my friends, and I told them all they had to do was be in it, and I would be the editor and the producer. I did that all of middle school." From a young age and without help or experience, Brooke was learning to come up with ideas, film videos, and edit them. All through middle school, Brooke continued producing music videos and uploading videos to her channel.

However, going into high school, Brooke decided to leave her music video hobby behind and "grow up." But she soon realized that "I missed it. YouTube was a way for me to express myself. I found a new pocket of the online world where people were doing makeup and fashion content, so I jumped into that. Even though I had no place of doing that." Outside of school hours, Brooke juggled her homework with planning and producing content and learning new ways to edit videos. And as YouTube trends have changed over the years, Brooke has stayed up with the differing content styles, adopting and changing her channel to what fits. "It has been different content geared toward different parts of my life."

In college, Brooke was still making videos and, during her senior year, started a podcast with her best friend and fellow YouTuber, Danielle Carolan. The two women started their podcast *Gals on the Go* in 2018, at the beginning of the emerging podcast craze. Podcast streaming on Spotify grew by 175 percent in 2018 (Music Ally, 2019). Brooke continued to see new opportunities for career growth, and even with a demanding course schedule, she made the time and put in the effort to work and do what she loved.

After graduating college, Brooke worked in a corporate job for a few months before ultimately deciding to make YouTube, social media, and podcasting her full-time job. After years of balancing school, friends, family, extracurriculars, and You-Tube, Brooke was in a financial position that allowed her to make her passion her career.

Brooke now lives in New York City, and year by year, is continuing to grow her platforms and engage with more followers who love her authenticity and relatable content, including myself. Reflecting on her path to get to where she is today, Brooke told me, "I never thought it would be my full-time thing. I always thought of it as just a hobby. Even going into college, I thought I would quit YouTube when I graduated. It was 2015, and no one had any idea of what YouTube would look like. It is so crazy how the vision of your life is so different from how it actually manifests to be."

When I asked Brooke about her advice to other young women, she said, "Say yes and do more stuff. Challenge yourself every day to get outside of your comfort zone and say yes." She herself lives by the motto, "Would you rather live with that desire, or would you rather try it and say I didn't like it, or at worse fail?"

I have said "yes" to many things in my life. Sometimes I enjoyed it and kept going, spin class, for instance, and sometimes I just said, "This isn't for me." (I quit softball after a few weeks.) All that matters is you just try and see how the shoe fits. Try more than once, try for a few weeks, but once you know in your heart that this isn't for you, go try something else! There are so many things to try, see, explore, do. So much out there that you have no idea exists.

You never know what life has in store for you. You never know what you might discover about yourself, where one "yes" will lead you. So just start saying "yes" and see where it takes you.

I know I will.

WHERE TO START:

Pick an activity

- What is one thing you have always wanted to try or one thing you want to start consistently doing? Maybe something you loved as a child but haven't had the opportunity to explore fully. Don't be afraid to try new things.

Make it a priority

- If something is important to you, you will find the time. Whatever you want to start doing, make it a priority. Schedule time for it in your day. Sign up for a class, so it feels more like an obligation. If money is involved, you are more likely to show up. Even if it is just one day a week. Commit to engaging with this activity and after a few weeks, see how you feel.

Hack your free time

- Every day, you have the same number of hours as everyone else. The same number of hours of people running multiple businesses, people with full-time jobs and families, full-time students with careers, and Beyoncé. I am not saying you need to run multiple businesses, work while being a student, or become Beyoncé. What I am saying is that it is entirely doable to use time to your advantage and get a lot done in a day. It is entirely doable to pursue a passion on the side and have a job. It is entirely doable to get all you need done and spend time focused on what you want and need. Use your hours and free time to your advantage.

When you open yourself up to new experiences and actively expand your horizons, you may discover new things that make you truly happy. And as you gradually move out of your comfort zone, you are also developing and strengthening your confidence muscle. Regardless of whether a passion becomes a hobby, career, or your purpose in life, pursuing something you are passionate about brings joy, happiness, and a renewed sense of meaning.

Nothing wrong with any of that!

CHAPTER 11

LIVING LIFE ON YOUR TERMS

———

"You have to choose between what the world expects of you and what you want for yourself."

—JAMES MCBRIDE; WRITER

You're browsing through social media and decide to check LinkedIn. We all know the feeling that comes after. For those of you that aren't familiar with this feeling, imagine scrolling through a feed of everyone posting about their accomplishments on a platform made for bragging. Sure, you are happy for everyone, but just like Instagram leaves you comparing your life to the people you follow, LinkedIn leaves you comparing your accomplishments, intelligence, and drive to those in your network. A seemingly harmless social media network for finding jobs leaves many with feelings of inadequacy, defeat, and stress.

Personally, I dread every time I go on LinkedIn because it is a reminder I am still jobless when everyone else I know has had a job secured since junior year.

The idea of getting a job postgraduation looms over college students the moment we move into our small shared dorm room. Which, in my case, was the worst dorm on campus, with the smallest rooms. I still loved it though.

From the moment we walk onto campus, we are surrounded by people constantly talking about jobs, internships, and grades. Not just our peers, but anyone, and everyone, when you say, "I am in college."

"Oh, you're in college. What are you doing when you graduate?"

"What internship do you have for the summer?"

"Did you get a return offer for next summer?"

"How are you doing in your classes?"

In a very simple form, college is four years of living with strangers who become friends, balancing a social life with trying to get good grades, and finding a job to brag about on LinkedIn.

Going into college, I was set on being a nutritionist. Before I even stepped onto campus, I already had my four years of classes planned out in a Google spreadsheet and a list of nutrition schools I had my eyes on. But after a rude awakening during an advising meeting freshmen year, where I learned I would need to complete a long list of med school requirements to be a nutritionist... I instantly changed my mind. So, I took inventory of my skillset, what I wanted in a job, and set my sights on a new career path.

While the vast majority of students at my school geared up to go to med school, work as an investment banker, become a consultant, or go into marketing, I wanted to plan parties—big, fun, colorful, extravagant parties.

From the get-go, my path was different than most, if not all, of my peers, and while I tried not to let it get to me, it was hard when everyone was constantly talking about recruiting, job interviews, and high-profile internships. For the majority of the school year, students' lives circulated around wearing business suits, attending networking event after networking event, prepping for interviews, and competing for the best internships, which would lead to full-time offers and brag-worthy LinkedIn posts.

I, on the other hand, did not interview anywhere, and when I did get an internship in event planning, it was unpaid, and I wore fun dresses and heels to work.

Although I had self-selected myself out of the club of business suit-clad students and those studying for graduate, law, and medical school, I felt like an outcast.

I felt unsuccessful compared to my peers, and quite frankly, a little embarrassed when they all asked what I wanted to do postgraduation. I'd bashfully tell them, "I want to be an event planner," feeling inferior because I wasn't pursuing a more prestigious job. I was unconventional, and doing the unconventional feels uncomfortable. It was a constant internal battle of "Am I doing the right thing by following my dreams, or am I shooting myself in the foot?"

At times I went back and forth, debating what I wanted to pursue and making countless pro and con lists. I researched, watched videos, inquired about different job industries, but at the end of the day, even with a pandemic that took a massive toll on the event industry, I kept coming back to the job that felt right to me. A job I knew from my internship experience made me excited to go to work every day.

I had to do what felt authentic to me, and that was going after a job that is not the most lucrative, not the most stable, not the most LinkedIn-worthy, but one that would make me excited to pursue.

I decided I don't want to live for what others expect me to do. I want to live for what I expect me to do.

CHOOSE YOURSELF

Katy had been pacing around her studio apartment all morning, rehearsing what she would later tell her boss—finding the right words felt crucial. Words that made her sound smart and like she knew what she was doing. Words that expressed her gratitude for the time, but she was now ready to go out on her own. Words that gave her the confidence this decision was the right one.

For the past eighteen months, Katy had worked as an assistant manager of digital and social content for a well-known beauty brand. But now, against the advice of her friends, parents, and peers, she decided to pursue her dream job working as a freelancer and growing her YouTube and podcast platforms.

Sitting in front of her boss with the endless opportunities of New York City just beyond the window, Katy proclaimed, "I am choosing myself," and quit.

While it doesn't have to be as dramatic as that, if there ever comes a time when you know in your heart that "this does not feel right," listen to it. You have to know when the right time to leave is, and just leave. The transition will be hard and have its fair share of ups and downs, but when you are on a path that feels authentic to you, in the end, all the trials and tribulations will be worth it.

When Katy knew she was ready for something more and excited by it, she decided it was time to leave. Although the adjustment was hard and Katy experienced ups and downs in the journey. With over 470,000 subscribers on YouTube, a highly rated podcast, and now her own graphic design business, I think it's safe to say she made a good decision.

I was fortunate to have had the opportunity to talk with Katy all about her career journey, from her humble beginnings on YouTube to now being her own boss and doing what she loves.

Katy started her YouTube channel in 2009 as a hobby, using the platform to find a sense of community. "I turned to making videos to kind of fake it till you make it in terms of coaching myself into being more confident, and that was my way to do that. Along with that, I wanted a community. I wanted to make friends because I didn't have many of them in my real life."

Throughout middle and high school, Katy was a victim of bullying. For her, "YouTube was the one thing I would look forward to after a day of getting stomped on and having people walk all over me and just use me in many different ways."

By 2011, at age sixteen, brands started contacting Katy for sponsored content and collaborations. What was once a fun hobby turned into a monetizable opportunity, which "at age sixteen is kind of a lot to wrap your head around." While taking classes and dealing with self-esteem issues, Katy signed with a manager and continued to work and grow her platform.

When Katy was a senior in college, she was in a unique position with a strong YouTube community and an already impressive resume. Katy had always known she wanted to work for herself, but with all of her peers accepting offers in illustrious jobs, Katy, too, felt the need to do the conventional.

"I took the job because I was like, okay, this company is a huge name. It's a beauty brand. Everyone knows it. So when people at parties or around the school would ask, 'What are you doing, after college?' I could impress them with the company. It sounds horrible, but I really took the job because it was safe to say, 'Oh, I'm working for this company.'"

The pressure and expectations she felt from her peers, parents, and followers to graduate and get a "real job" swayed Katy's decision. She chose to follow the expectations of her instead what she wanted for herself. "I was worried my followers would think I was less relatable. If after these four years of college, I put them through on all my social media platforms, me being like, 'Oh yeah, I got this degree, and I'm doing nothing with it.' I wanted to remain relatable."

Katy did what garnered the approval of others. She moved to NYC, moved to her new apartment, and moved into her corporate lifestyle.

But, Katy didn't put her dreams on hold. On Sundays, Katy would sit down for dinner, her iPad, next to her so she could try out the world of graphic designing. Practicing new layouts and designs whenever she could. She continued to record podcasts and produce videos for her YouTube channel. She was producing content that brought her followers into her new phase of life and provided advice and comfort to those also transitioning from college to corporate. Even though her time was pulled elsewhere, she continued to work at her craft, the thing she loved, whenever possible.

Even if you have to pursue one career to make ends meet, that does not mean you cannot work on your passions alongside it. Katy's job allowed her to make ends meet and learn all about creating content in the beauty industry. But Katy's dream job was ultimately starting her own design business. When Katy had the time, she worked on her passions. If Katy didn't have the time, she made the time by staying up late to finish a video or waking up early to record a podcast. Although Katy didn't know when the magic time would come where she could pursue her passions full-time, she kept dedicating time toward building a design portfolio for when that time would come.

After eighteen months of a lot of learning, growing, and confidence-building, Katy made the decision to finally go after her dreams on her terms.

"[When I decided to quit, I was worried] I would be letting people down, and I never really thought to myself, well, if I stay, I am letting myself down. I'm the biggest factor in whether or not I'm happy and content, and I had all the power in my hands to figure that out. I had all the power to decide if I wanted to leave. Luckily I finally came to my senses." Although Katy loved her company and her team, something told her where she was and what she was doing wasn't meant for her.

"The biggest mantra I stand by is that if you find yourself in the wrong story, you have to leave. I was having fun in the story, but I didn't feel like it was me living it. I felt like I was on the outside watching this person named Katy go to work every day, but it wasn't me."

Katy came to the decision to quit her job. "It was really hard [to quit my job], but looking back a year later, I am so relieved I did it when I did, and I didn't just stick around because it was easier and more comfortable to remain somewhere you're unhappy versus having a hard conversation with your boss, with yourself, with every person that asks you afterward why you left."

Although at first, it was daunting to adjust to her new life as her own boss, one day at a time, Katy worked on developing and improving her brand. A year after she quit and started her own business, Katy had a full list of clients, with new projects needing to be turned away due to lack of time.

Many of us likely have dreams and ideas for our futures that don't necessarily fit the norm or comply with expectations imposed on us. And like Katy originally did, we sacrifice letting ourselves down to pursue what garners approval from others. Even as a social media influencer with the platform and financial ability to pursue her dream job full-time, she too felt pressure to follow the expectations set for her.

I am of the belief that expectations, comparison, and caring about other's opinions over your own are the three most dangerous things to our inner peace. And as Elizabeth George wrote, "Expectations destroy our peace of mind. They are future disappointments, planned out in advance."

We are not available to listen or trust ourselves when we get our information from the outside instead of from within.

Let go of others expectation baggage. It will make your journey smoother.

UNLEARNING HELPLESSNESS

Learned helplessness is a state that occurs after an individual has continuously experienced a stressful situation. Because they have faced the negative situation repeatedly, they come to believe that they are unable to control or change the situation, so they do not try—even when they have the abilities to change, or new opportunities present themself. The perception that the situation is out of their control, that there is nothing they can do, causes the individual to become passive and allow the behavior to keep occurring. Typically, learned helplessness presents as a lack of self-esteem, low motivation, a lack of perseverance, giving up, and frustration (Cherry, 2021).

For example, someone who is not comfortable in social situations and feels shy may start to feel that there is nothing they can do to overcome this feeling. They believe their symptoms are out of their control and eventually stop trying to engage in social situations altogether. In turn, this makes their shyness more pronounced and increases the discomfort they feel (Cherry, 2021).

Another example of learned helplessness is someone who is feeling the effects of aging. Someone who is aging may feel like there is nothing they can do to combat the aging process. While getting older is a natural part of life, there are many things one can do to slow down the aging process and help one age better. These include: eating well, doing strength exercises, walking, drinking plenty of water, and doing math or memory problems to help your brain. Even though there is so much out of our control, we can always do little things to take back some control or at least make our situations better off.

When we are helpless and believe that we have no control over our lives, we forget all the things we can control to make things better and point us in the right direction. When we are helpless, we don't make an effort to act and change, so nothing does. When we are helpless, our mindset holds us back from seeing new opportunities or realizing our abilities.

However, in any situation, it is always possible to take action and make a change. We are never truly stuck. We are only stuck if we believe nothing can or will change. Things can and will change. You just have to be open to seeing new possibilities.

THERE IS NO GOLDEN TIME

You might not graduate and move to your dream city and do your dream job. You might not know what you want to do. You might not have the financial ability to pursue certain careers. You might have other hurdles that prevent you from going all-in on your dreams. Whatever the case is for you, if you are lucky enough to have one or two things you love to do, that give you energy and you can do for a job, hold onto those gifts and don't forget that they are worth exploring. It might take time. It might take practice and refining your skills like Katy did. It might take going down different career paths to make money, gain experience, learn a new craft or skill. But when the time is right, trust yourself and make the leap.

If your dream isn't realistic at the moment, there are still things you can do to make it happen for you in the future:

- **Be in the vicinity of your interests**. Surround yourself with others doing what you want to do. If you want to be an actress, try a class or audition for a community theater. If you want to be a doctor, start volunteering at hospitals.

If you want to be a therapist, get your own therapist. If you love to bake, start finding your best recipes and sharing your goodies with friends. "Getting in the vicinity" of your interests is a great way to allow your skills to develop while keeping an open mind to where they can lead you.

- **Make connections.** Reach out to people who are in a job that you want. Ask them for coffee, learn more about the job, ask them questions about their career journey. If you connect, there's a chance they may become a sounding board for your ideas or a mentor to you in the future.

- **Practice in your free time.** Depending on your dream job: start drawing up designs, going to auditions, performing at open mic nights, taking practice tests, writing short stories, creating mockups. Read about your industry and learn as much as possible. Build your experience and portfolio to make you stand out from the get-go.

And as with anything, mindset is everything. Thinking back on her experience, Katy told me, "There's really no pressure to start out right off the bat. Looking back, I wish I would have had a little more faith in myself to be a freelancer, but I still do think that if I could go back and do it again, I would still take the beauty brand job, but with a different mindset. Thinking 'I'm not taking this job because I don't think I could survive in any other way' but taking it as a means to support myself for a bit, to learn new things, knowing it was tough, but knowing that it could be something temporary, it could be a steppingstone."

No matter where you are in life, what you are doing, who you are with, you know the answers. "You have to trust your gut and trust your feelings. There is no golden time."

Ultimately, you have to choose what you envision for yourself over what others choose for you.

. . .

"Listen to your own voice, your own soul. Too many people listen to the noise of the world instead of themselves."

—Leon Brown

. . .

PART FOUR:

LEARNING

CHAPTER 12

MOVING THROUGH FEAR

"Each of us must confront our own fears, must come face to face with them. How we handle our fears will determine where we go with the rest of our lives. To experience adventure or to be limited by the fear of it."

—JUDY BLUME; WRITER

It looked like a prison when I first saw it—just one huge concrete building slap in the middle of Cambridge, MA. Luckily the building was covered with huge windows, making it feel a little more... welcoming. To go from walking through Harvard's quad, with all the beautiful brick buildings, to crossing the street and seeing my new high school, "the prison," a school I was unfamiliar with and knew no one at, was a bit unsettling, to say the least.

It was my first day of school, but this first day was unlike any I had experienced before. It was my first day of sophomore year, in a new country, a new city, a new school, a new world. Just a few weeks prior, my family drove up to our new house—a blue Victorian with a bright pink door that I like to refer to as "Barbie's dream house." Together we walked through the front door, greeted by boxes waiting to be unpacked and ready to make our house a home.

It had been eight years since we had lived in the US, and everything was new and different, including the selection of yogurts at our nearest grocery store. For the past eight years, we lived in a small suburban town called Egham in England. My brother and I attended a private international school just a mile down the road. The school was primarily made up of expats, kids whose parents' jobs took them to different countries quite frequently. Friends moving away and new kids starting was so normal that it became a competition between the friend groups to adopt any new kid into their clique. No one had to try hard to make friends, to belong. Students were instantly welcoming to new kids. On day one of second grade, when we first moved there, I had friends. From day one, it was easy, and I seemed to fit in.

The size of my grade from second grade to freshman year of high school was fifty students. We all knew everything about each other, including everyone's parents, siblings, and intimate life details. The small grade also meant that we all dated the same people. My ex-middle school boyfriend became my best friend's next boyfriend, and for some reason, that just was not weird to us—when it should have been! From day one, I felt safe, comfortable, and free to be myself. But eight years later, with my brother attending college in the fall at Northeastern, it was time to move back to our original home country.

Moving back to the states was exciting... in theory. I dreamed of attending football games with my friends, getting dolled up to go to homecoming, and going to fun parties on the weekends. In reality, it was nothing like my imagination or the movies.

Walking into the large double doors that first day, my heart was beating out of my chest. I had spent the past two days perfecting the perfect outfit, a mid-thigh light blue dress with tiny white flowers and sleeves that tied into bows at the shoulder, paired with white sandals, a light cream cardigan, and loose brown curls that cascaded down my shoulders. I wanted to make a good impression but what I quickly realized as I made my way down the crowded locker-lined hallways was that I was out of my element. I was immediately surrounded by a swarm of students filling the halls as shrieks bounced off the walls from friends seeing each other after the long summer. I thought I was ready, but all I felt was lost, alone, and unprepared. The only thing I had prepared was my outfit and shoulder bag full of colorful pens and notepads, making it weigh about five pounds on my right arm.

When I finally found the classroom printed on the paper slip I carried, I entered to see students sitting in different parts of the room, already in formed cliques, uninterested in anything other than the gossip they were sharing. I walked in, unnoticed, confronted with the reality that for the first time in my life, I had to put myself out there to meet people, to make friends.

That scared the *shit* out of me.

I took the seat at the front of the room as nerves bubbled from within, making me oddly very hot and cold at the same time.

A new school is one thing, but a new school sophomore year in a place where everyone grew up together is another. Everyone already had established friend groups, clubs they were interested in, sports teams they played on, teachers they knew to take and which ones not to take. I didn't even know the locations of the bathrooms. I was insecure and unsure of who I was and how the US public school system worked. Was it like the movies where mean girl cliques fueled their conversations by cruel gossip? How did people make friends? Is it weird if I ask someone to get lunch? What if they say no? If people know who I am, would they say bad things about me?

I didn't want to be talked poorly about. I didn't want to step on anyone's toes. I didn't want to make anyone uncomfortable. I was so afraid of being too much or making a bad impression that I became small. I was so afraid of what would happen if I put myself out there that I hid. From day one, I made myself unnoticeable. I attended class, I spoke when I was called on or asked a question, but I never made an effort to make friends, reach out, or be seen. At lunch, I ate alone, on the fourth-floor hallway, away from anyone who would see me. After school, I walked back out through the double doors and straight home while everyone gathered with their friends outside.

In the afternoons, while people went over to their friends' houses or met up in Harvard Square, I did schoolwork in the kitchen while my mom cooked and worked on her design projects. On the weekends, I worked at the desk in the living room, spending time with my family when I needed a break. During my last three years of high school, I never attended homecoming, I went to three football games (we weren't good at football anyways), and I made only one friend. For three years, I let fear and my insecurities dictate how I lived my life.

I prevented myself from being seen or known because I feared what people would say about me and how I would be perceived. I was afraid if I spoke up in class, I would get the wrong answer—I was mentally scarred from the time I read out loud in class and pronounced militia as "mill-e-tea-a." I let the fear of rejection hold me back from asking someone to get lunch and potentially make a new friend. I didn't try to join clubs, speak up, win awards because if I didn't try, I couldn't fail. I couldn't face rejection.

I let fear take over and convince me to play everything safe, only following my rigid rules and plans, not being spontaneous, or letting myself truly live in the moment. I let my fear diminish my abilities, keeping me constrained in a safe little box that gave me a false sense of control. I never had full control; we hardly ever do. But that little safe box I made for myself allowed me to feel like I had everything figured out. As long as I did x and didn't do y, everything would work out the way I wanted it to.

It never did work the way I imagined.

In high school, I wanted to lose weight, so I counted calories and worked out to get to my goal. I didn't eat more calories than I should have, and I didn't take rest days. I did the x (calorie count and exercise) and didn't do the y (eat too much or not move enough). But instead of getting the body of my dreams and having everything magically fall into place, I became obsessive, detached, and sad. My false sense of control was a result of being able to control the things I could (me) and eliminating the things I couldn't control (people and experiences). My safe box didn't give me the life I wanted. Instead, it separated me from the woman I want to be and the life I want to live.

So, what did put me on the path to becoming the woman I want to be?

Escaping the safe box I made for myself.

Escaping the box made me confident, poised, and inspired. Escaping the box helped me truly live and find who I am. Escaping the box started when I decided to write this book.

ESCAPING THE BOX

I decided to finally escape my box when I looked back and realized what I had missed out on because I got in the way. The countless times I had met someone I liked, but because of my fear of "being too much" or "not being wanted," I didn't try to become their friend or ask them to hang out. All the times I walked through the halls and saw someone I knew, but my protection mechanism told me to pick up my phone and look at it instead of giving them a genuine smile. The plans I turned down because I was afraid of putting myself out there. I even turned down a party that Malia Obama attended. If that was not a wake-up call to stop holding myself back from meeting people and having fun, I don't know what is.

For so many years, I have cared way too much about what others think about me. I have cared way too much about being liked, doing the "right thing," and acting the "right" way. When I look back on the times I've had my favorite experiences, met my best friends, created the best memories and stories, they are the moments I let go and just lived. The times I didn't hold myself back from putting myself out there. The times I said yes to plans and fully enjoyed the present moment, not stressed about what was coming next. When I let go of control, took down my walls, and let people see the real me.

There are billions of people on this planet and endless opportunities. I no longer wanted to live my life doing everything "safe." I wanted to enjoy the world, meet different people, experience all that I could in this life. After years of living a controlled life and playing everything safe, I decided I had enough of living life fearfully.

So, I let down my walls and wrote this book—a book that details my vulnerabilities and insecurities. A book I have no control over once it is in the hands of a reader. A book that takes my fears of rejection and judgment and says, "Here, read this, and then rate and review."

Not everyone will like this book, not everyone will like me, and after so many years, I have decided that is okay.

COURAGE IS FEAR'S WORST ENEMY, BUT YOUR NEW BEST FRIEND

Whenever we want to do something big or scary, we usually ask ourselves: *What if the worst possible imaginable thing happens? What if I embarrass myself? What if I mess up? What If I lose? What if I get rejected? What if they say no?* And if we want to begin a creative project, open our own business, pursue a passion, we tend to think *I am not qualified for this. I am an imposter.*

I had to face that fear when writing this book. I don't have all the answers. I don't have my life figured out. While I have faced challenging times in my life (and still do), I know so many women who are more qualified than I am to tackle these topics. So many women with deeper life stories than mine. Women with big platforms and followings who could reach huge audiences with their books and make an impact. I'm not qualified, heck I only took one English class in college, I have a very small following on Instagram, and I have not done or founded anything revolutionary. But after a year of mental back and forth deciding if I should write this book,

I realized I am qualified because I am a human, and I have stories and experiences to share. I am not an imposter because I am not pretending to be someone I am not. Even though I have never done anything exceptional or faced deep traumas, I still have wisdom that may be helpful. Although there are thousands of books like this in the market, none exist from my point of view with my words. If I want to write a book, I should, because I can.

We all have a voice and ideas for a reason. We are meant to share what is in our hearts and our heads. We are meant to create things, chase fantasies, generate new ideas, let our imagination go wild. I know it can be easier said than done, but just think of all the things that could have been created but weren't because someone didn't have the confidence to start something or felt it had already been done. What if Thomas Edison didn't pursue the idea of electricity? What if Neil Armstrong thought the idea of walking on the moon was impossible? What if Jeff Bezos decided there were already too many people in the digital market? What if someone didn't question if there were other planets or if the earth wasn't flat? Without people having the courage to allow their imagination to go where it wants to, to create what it wants to, we wouldn't have all the incredible inventions and knowledge we have today.

I am confident when I say no matter if you win or lose, fail, or succeed, embarrass yourself or impress yourself, you will gain something, whether that be a friendship, confidence, or even just a good story. In my times of losing, feeling stuck, facing embarrassment, I have gained an invaluable lesson of what to do next time or how to change moving forward. I gained humility and more assurance in myself.

Even when I have failed, I have won because I tried, and life is not about playing things safe and living life in a box. We all have one life. We are all blessed and lucky to be given an opportunity to make a mark on the world and those around us. We are supposed to try and fail. We are supposed to feel fear but rise above regardless. You will never know what can come out of trying, of saying "yes" when fear is saying "You aren't capable."

Fear will never go away, it will always be there, but when you act, fear will recede because you have shown it your power. If we hold ourselves back and don't do things because of fear, we are not living life for ourselves or our dreams. We are living our fears.

In his book *The War of Art*, Steven Pressfield writes, "Most of us have two lives. The life we live, and the un-lived life within us." Which life will you choose, the life you actually want, or one shaped by fear? I used to live my life in fear, but this book… this is my catalyst to living life without fear. After all, I am putting my whole life out there for people to read about, judge, compare, and reject.

In the end, you have two choices: face your fears or avoid them and never reach your full potential. Choose wisely.

WE ALL HAVE FEARS

When I asked my friends and family their biggest fears, these were some responses I got:

- Earthquakes
- Being used
- Not being enough

- Rejection
- Prison
- Being overlooked
- Losing people I love
- Loneliness
- Lack of control in a situation
- Being trapped
- Humiliation

Many people said the same fears, and many could not choose just one.

Fears are in our DNA. They are what help keep us alive and protect us from legitimate threats. Many are there for a biological reason, to help keep us alive and spot danger. While other fears may seem "irrational." Regardless of what your fear is, we all have them.

Although I was unable to interview her, in a speech at Harvard's graduation, Oprah Winfrey admitted she is scared of balloons, telling the crowd: "I really don't like balloons, I don't like balloons!"

So when Oprah's entire staff surprised her with an entire audience filled with balloons for her fortieth birthday, Oprah could only do one thing: confront her fear. And she did just that by walking through a sea of ready-to-burst latex decorations (Saad, 2013).

In a promotional video for *O Magazine*, Oprah, then fifty-nine, looked back on that day, she said, "There are a few things that in life if you allow them to, can really keep you from moving forward." For Oprah, when faced with her fear, there was "no way around it—[I] just had to walk through them."

Next time you find yourself face to face with your fear, try channeling Oprah and walk right through it.

HOW I TRY TO LIVE WITHOUT FEAR:

1. Write it out, work it out

The first step to living without fear controlling you is recognizing what you are fearful of. For some, this is easy to pinpoint. For others, this might take a while and require reflection time and reaching inward. For me, it helps to write it down, to journal and sit with myself in a quiet area and just think. This might not work for you. We are all different. What is important here is that you give yourself the chance to reflect and understand what you are fearful of and why. Fear has legs and arms. Fear is attached to other things you might not be conscious of. Get to know your fear. The better informed and aware you are, the better chance you are to overcome it at its root.

For me, my fear of rejection has legs in my ideal to be as perfect as I can be. It has arms in comparing myself to others and feeling inadequate about myself. It has legs in feeling like I am not good enough, pretty enough, smart enough, interesting enough. I was not afraid of rejection itself. I was afraid if I put myself out there and got rejected, that meant I was not worthy, and even though I tried so hard to be and look a certain way, all the effort was not worth it. I was not worth it.

It took time, but once I realized my fears and their roots, I understood more about myself and why I act in certain ways.

2. Decide that you want to live the un-lived life within you

As I mentioned above, you have two choices: live your life with fear and accept that you won't be reaching your full potential, or live your life with the goal of overcoming your fears and being true to what you want, despite labels and challenges. Decide how you want to live your life and what potential you want to achieve. Make a choice for yourself. Forget the circumstances, your living situation, your bank account, your credentials, or anything else that puts you into a category and a box. What do you want?

3. Take a step back

Facing your fears does not have to happen overnight, or as soon you recognize what it is that is holding you back. Change and growth do not happen in a day, nor should they. Take your time. Do not rush or put pressure on yourself. The most important part is that you are aware and want to take back your power. Give yourself a goal if that will help you. Confide in a loved one or acquaintance if that will keep you accountable. Allow yourself space to feel the fear and feel the fire that you need to confront that fear.

Think of it like a puzzle where you have no idea what the final image will be. You don't just start doing the puzzle right away. You take a step back and look at all the pieces. You spend a few minutes examining each piece, identifying the pieces that make up the boundaries.

At times it's frustrating, and you want to give up, but then you see patterns and connections form. Once you get a rhythm going, excitement builds, and with each piece you put together, you are making more and more progress. Depending on your experience and the level of difficulty, it might take hours or even days to finish the puzzle. But the most important part is to never give up. When things get hard, all you need to do is take a step back and dedicate time to just sitting there examining it. Building a puzzle is not a race. It is not about speed. Puzzles are about determination. It's a game of patience and working toward the big picture.

4. Baby steps are okay

It doesn't have to happen at once. It can be helpful to go full throttle but if that does not feel true to you, take the smaller strides. Each step you take is a success within itself. However, if it's the fear of jumping out of a plane, that kind of requires a big jump.

5. Say goodbye

When you are ready, and sometimes even before you are fully ready, go out there and live your life in spite of fear. Do not let fear run the show anymore. It is time to start living for you. Fear will always be there; it never goes away, and new ones come up all the time. But if you keep taking action for yourself and not for your fear, I can promise you that your life will get bigger and feel lighter.

6. Remember

It doesn't get easier. It is not just you. Everyone, even the people who in our minds are "perfect" or "have made it," has fears *every single day.* There is no one size fits all approach to fear. Fears have different magnitudes, they come, and they go. Some we will never be able to overcome, some we may be able to face, but that doesn't mean they will go away. Fear will always be with you. I just hope you can learn to listen more to your inner self and recognize them when they come. I hope you know how powerful you are and how much you can achieve, even if people say otherwise. I hope if a fear is holding you back from going after something you want or starting something that is meaningful to you, you won't listen anymore.

CHAPTER 13

LABELS, THOUGHTS, BELIEFS, OH MY!

"Thoughts have power; thoughts are energy. And you can make your world or break it by your own thinking."

—SUSAN TAYLOR; AMERICAN EDITOR,
FORMER EDITOR-IN-CHIEF OF *ESSENCE*

I could almost smell the freshly baked pastries as I scrolled through my camera roll, looking at pictures from my 2017 trip to Paris—trying to relive the good times when I did not live in leggings twenty-four seven. As I clicked through each picture, I was instantly transported back into that moment. I could taste the crunch of the buttery croissants as I walked through the gorgeous Parisian streets on tree-lined sidewalks painted with shadows of leaves. Then, looking through memories from my spring break in the Caribbean, I heard the crash of the ocean waves and felt the hot air on my skin. I was overcome with nostalgia looking at the hundreds of selfies from my junior year abroad. I smiled at pictures from college nights out and faded memories that mostly consisted of lots and lots of dancing (and sweating) with my friends.

While my trip down memory lane made my heart flutter with happiness and longing for times like those again, it also brought back the negative feelings I had in those moments. The times in Paris when I would walk around silently counting calories in my head or bashing myself for eating too much bread at lunch. The time when I silently cried for an hour in my bikini because I caught a glimpse of myself in the mirror and hated what I saw. The pictures that were taken that I would continuously zoom in on, nitpicking every flaw. The pictures where I was smiling on the outside, but deep down, I was struggling.

As I looked through those pictures, I saw something completely different than I had at the moment. I saw how skinny I looked in Paris when at the time, I thought I was "fat." How cute I looked in my red bikini. How healthy and radiant I looked in the pictures I had torn apart years before.

The problem was never how I looked, where I was, or what I was doing. The problem was my inner critic, my negative self-talk.

We experience the world through a lens that our thoughts have molded. Our perceptions of ourselves, others, and the world are shaped by the stories we tell ourselves. The basis of our reality is not on actual truth. Rather, it is created based on what we perceive to be accurate and true.

The negative self-talk that I wasn't good enough, wasn't skinny enough, and wasn't pretty enough made me see myself and my capabilities through a clouded lens. I believed the story in my head, and that is how I saw and lived my life.

We all partake in this kind of negative self-talk from time to time. As humans, we tend to think about negative events much more than positive events. This is because of how our brains are wired—likely as part of our evolutionary need to avoid danger. Psychologists refer to this phenomenon as negativity bias. Because of our bias toward the negative, a bad event has a much more pronounced and powerful impact on our brain, so we pay more attention (Cherry, 2020). Even if there were many positives in your day, one bad thing—such as your boss getting mad at you for missing a meeting—can make you forget all of the good moments and focus solely on the bad.

But even though our brain has this bias, we are ultimately still in control of our thoughts. In order to combat the negativity bias, we have to practice consciously bringing uplifting thoughts to the forefront of our awareness.

I know I am not alone in being my own worst critic and allowing my head to rule how I see the world. I am constantly working on catching my critic and putting her in her place! To be honest, as I sit here typing this chapter, I have deeply struggled with negative self-talk this past week.

What has helped me in the past that I will continue to practice is actively being aware of my thoughts. Tuning into the stories I am telling myself, the labels I give myself, and the words I choose to describe a situation. Our thoughts are powerful. They influence how we see the world and how we see ourselves. We can reframe our thoughts and choose our words, and when we do, we change who we become.

· · ·

"A man is the product of his thoughts. What he thinks, he becomes"

—*Mahatma Gandhi*

· · ·

CHOOSING THE RIGHT LABELS

I am lazy.

I am an introvert.

I hate exercise.

I am not a good driver.

I don't like reading.

I am not creative.

I can't lose weight.

I am not good at math.

I am a bad cook.

I am a bad dancer.

I am bad with money.

I am sure you have probably labeled yourself at least one of those in the past. I, for one, declared that "I don't like reading" for twenty-one years of my life. I tied myself so tightly to the idea that I did not like to read that I never bothered to try it outside of academia... or really inside academia. Yep, I am guilty of looking at the CliffNotes for 90 percent of the books I had to read for school. I only started actually enjoying reading when I picked up a book that interested me and realized, "Hey, this is great." As it turns out, I discovered I love to read! In the past four months, I have read twenty-five books—more books than I had read in my entire life.

As humans, we love labels. Labels make things concrete. Labels give us context and boundaries. Labels set expectations. Labels reveal a lot in just a few words. Labeling someone "an athlete" makes us think a person is strong, fit, determined, motivated, healthy, powerful. Just that one label gives us an idea of who they may be. The label of a "vegan" tells you a person doesn't consume or wear animal products. We may also speculate this person is passionate about health, the environment, and animal rights, which gives us more clues into how they live. Whether we are aware of it or not, labels have power in the way we view others and, perhaps more importantly, ourselves.

If you have labeled yourself as "lazy," what kind of actions and lifestyle followed that? Did you get up early and workout, or did you spend most of your day avoiding the activities you knew would be good for you? That label, that belief about who you were, played a role in creating your laziness. It was not a trait you were born with. It was a thought you had and thus shaped your behavior.

I worked at a restaurant with a guy who told me he was lazy from the moment we met. On our first shift together as servers, I asked him how his weekend was. He replied, "I am lazy, so I didn't do much."

He and I attended the same rigorous college. Clearly, he couldn't be that lazy if he was able to get into that school. And yet, because he thought of himself as being lazy, he lived the lifestyle of a lazy person. Most days, he would sleep until one or two in the afternoon, waking up just in time for his classes. During his free moments, he would play video games, and on the few occasions we would study together, he would leave after an hour. He would even skip meals because the seven-minute walk to the dining hall was too long.

He was not born lazy. He can be incredibly productive, but most of the time, his belief that he is lazy, holds him back and becomes the story about himself that he makes into his reality.

When we label ourselves, we box ourselves in and set ourselves up with expectations, beliefs, and boundaries.

Often, putting positive labels on ourselves seems much harder. It is easier to label yourself as "lazy" rather than "motivated" because it feels safer. When we say we are a "bad driver," nobody expects us to drive well, so we release the pressure and expectations. The danger is we start to believe we can't drive. We now have a story in our head that we can't drive, leading us to feel anxious while driving and possibly resisting it altogether. I used to call myself a "bad driver," and for months, I avoided getting behind the wheel. Finally, I let go of this idea and replaced it with a more positive label: "I am a safe driver." Suddenly I became more comfortable behind the wheel and more willing to drive.

The labels we give ourselves can motivate or demotivate us. Saying "I am not good at sports" might discourage you from trying sports or working out in general. But calling yourself "active" would inspire you to get more involved in fitness and live the lifestyle of a fit person. Once you realize you can call yourself an athlete, an artist, a cook, a dancer—whatever engages you. If you're actively participating in the activity, it gets easier to add positive labels.

Whatever the label is, once we start feeding our mind with that idea, we adopt it, reinforce it, and act in accordance with it. Our thoughts shape who we become, and our labels give us an idea about who we are.

Recently, I have made it a point to make conscious decisions about my labels for myself, choosing only positive labels and avoiding any that lock me into a certain way of being.

My labels as of now are:

I am a woman.

I am a student.

I am a daughter, a sister, a friend.

I am half American and half Italian.

I am creative.

I am a reader.

I am an avid walker and traveler.

I am an exercise enthusiast.

I am balanced.

I am strong.

I am motivated, focused, and grounded.

I am a first-time author.

These labels are parts of who I am, and they uplift me and allow me to express myself. I do not feel confined to a box or a particular way of being. I also made sure none of my labels declare what I am not.

Do this activity yourself! Make a list of all labels you have used to describe yourself, both in the past and in the present. Write them all down and read them back to yourself. Once you are done, get rid of any labels that don't serve you. Get rid of any belief of who you are that holds you back from being who you could be—who you want to be. Give yourself new labels if that helps, too. But always choose your labels carefully because the labels we choose influence our behavior, thoughts, lifestyle, and actions. Our labels influence our reality.

CHANGING OLD STORIES

We don't just create narratives about ourselves. We also do this to other people in our lives.

My brother, Max, is three years older than I am and, for the majority of my childhood, a pain in my ass. Growing up with an older brother usually means lots of teasing and protectiveness, which I got. But I also got someone who put me down quite a bit.

I started wearing makeup in the seventh grade. On school mornings, I would spend a good thirty minutes caking makeup on my face, going the full nine yards as if every day were picture day. I would come downstairs, makeup on point (or so I thought at the time), hair stick straight (because I had not yet appreciated my natural waves), with an Abercrombie getup to complete the 2010 middle school starter pack. My brother would immediately look at me in disgust and tell me to go wash my face.

When a thirteen-year-old spends an hour in the morning working to look a certain way and feel beautiful, hearing "Take it off" felt like a slap in the face.

At dinners or anytime we were together as a family, I felt silenced. My brother drew all attention to him. Dinners were the "Max Show": what Max did that day, how well he was doing in school or his job, what new entrepreneurial efforts he was embarking on. Whenever I tried to add to the conversation, I couldn't finish a thought without him pulling the conversation back to himself. My parents would try their best to focus on me, but somehow, Max always found a way to get his stories in. It was maddening.

To this day, I harbor resentment toward him. I love him, don't get me wrong. And I know he has immensely grown since we were living in the same house. But I continue to tell myself a story that he is not generous. He is not kind. He is a mooch. He doesn't say anything positive to me. The labels I put on him may also be entirely different from the labels my extended family has given him or how his friends have labeled him. Everyone has a different perspective. But whether my story has truth to it or not, it is not serving me, and it is not serving our relationship. In order to begin to build a stronger sibling bond, I need to tell myself a new story. I need to replace the past negatives with new positives. I need to change my story because whatever story I choose to tell, that is the life I will live. Those are the relationships I will form.

I realize I have done this with other people in my life: friends, boyfriends, roommates. I have held onto an old version of someone, a past experience. I have forgiven but not forgotten. But this has not gotten me anywhere. All it has done is cause me to carry extra weight in my heart and in my head. All it has done is hold me back from moving forward and improving my relationships.

People change—they really can, and they really do. I know that they have changed—why can't I let them? Why can't I let go of the old stories? I can, I should, and I will.

I will because I don't want to live with resentment or pain. I want to live with hope. I want to live with positivity. I want to live with an open mind and heart.

It starts with changing my story.

Recently I worked to let go of my old stories surrounding my brother, and I can honestly say we got closer, and our relationship improved—he even came to visit me at college for a weekend.

. . .

"The world as we have created it is a process of our thinking. It cannot be changed without changing our thinking."

—Albert Einstein

. . .

IT'S ALL ABOUT ENERGY

We are energetic beings. Everything we see, hear, feel, touch, and smell is energy. Our thoughts are energy. Our actions are energy. Our behavior is energy. Even seemingly empty spaces are full of energy (Hurst, 2019).

In this sense, we are all connected.

I do not want to get too scientific you, for both of our sakes. But I do want to make sure we are on the same page (no book pun intended).

Everything, whether you can see it or not, is moving. Even solid objects, like the book you are holding and your kitchen table, are moving. All matter consists of microscopic atoms and particles that are constantly vibrating. Frequency is the rate at which the vibrations occur, and each vibration has its own frequency. An atom that is moving at a faster rate operates at a higher frequency than an atom moving at a slower rate (Sessums, 2020).

As humans, we want to be operating at a higher (positive) frequency. And, according to the philosophy of the Law of Attraction, positive thoughts and energy attract positive results, while negative thoughts lead to negative outcomes (Scott, 2020). The overall principle is: like attracts like. When we raise our vibrations, we are attracting higher vibrations back to us.

We can change our vibrational frequencies by changing our thoughts. Different thoughts carry different vibrations. Happiness comes from high-frequency thoughts, while jealousy comes from low-frequency thoughts. Negative self-talk and insecurity lower our vibrational frequencies, while gratitude and positive affirmations can increase vibrational frequencies. The feeling of love is the highest frequency you can emit (Stanborough, 2020).

According to Dr. Fred Luskin at Stanford University, the average person has over sixty thousand thoughts a day. Ninety percent of which are exactly the same as the day before. And it has been found that, of those thoughts, 60–70 percent are negative (Raghunathan, 2013). If we want to be in a higher vibe, to attract better things to us, and to feel generally better, we need to be conscious of the thoughts we think.

In *The Secret,* a best-selling book on the Law of Attraction, the author, Rhonda Byrne, writes: "Your feelings are the primary tool that will help create your life. Your thoughts are the primary cause of everything." If you want to tap into your thoughts, your feelings are a good place to start.

PEOPLE REMEMBER HOW YOU MADE THEM FEEL

Not only do our thoughts affect our energy levels and what we attract in our lives, but our thoughts can also affect others around us. Our negative thoughts have the potential to bring others' energy down or push them away. We have all undoubtedly noticed how someone who is kind, fun, and joyful can come into a group, and suddenly everyone seems to just perk up. That one person can cause the energy to brighten and buzz in the room.

When someone we are with is in a positive state, they emit a strong vibrational frequency that can increase our energy and leave us feeling good. In contrast, if someone is not in a good state, the energy they emit is low and can lower our vibration. I don't know about you, but I can automatically feel a negative shift in the room if someone enters who is not having a good day. They may not know it, but their energy affects others around them because they are quite literally causing a change in our collective energies.

There was a girl who went to my summer camp named Olivia. Every time I saw Olivia, she was always smiling and seemingly in a good mood. Being around her felt good, energetic, and happy. I remember coming back from camp and telling my family all about my summer, recounting all the great memories I had, all the fun stuff I did, all the PB&J sandwiches I ate (probably twenty). I told them all about my friends, and I told them about Olivia. "There was this girl at camp, Olivia. She was always happy, always smiling, and whenever you were around her, you felt good. I want to be like her." My grandma still remembers what I said and even reminds me to this day.

I will always remember Olivia and how she made me feel. Olivia was a high-vibration person. Love and joy radiated from her, positively affecting those in her presence. I wanted to be like Olivia then, and I want to be like her now.

· · ·

"At the end of the day, people won't remember what you said or did, they will remember how you made them feel."

—*Maya Angelou*

· · ·

Maybe all of us can aspire to be a little like Olivia.

But the reality is we can't always be in a high vibrational place. And that is okay. It is okay to be in a stuck place, okay to feel sad or lonely. But when we are ready to move through our feelings, ready to start operating at a higher vibe, we can begin by directing our thoughts and feelings, one step at a time.

MOVING TO A HIGHER VIBRATION

The author and inspirational speaker Esther Hicks has created the emotional guidance scale. It's a scale of commonly felt emotions ranging from joy, freedom, and love as the highest vibrational emotions, and depression, grief, and despair as the lowest. This guide is a helpful tool to lift ourselves from our current emotional place to one with a higher vibration.

When you are feeling down and negative, trying to think high-energy thoughts can feel forced and inauthentic. The idea of the scale is that we can't go from one side of the scale to the other—the big leap between low and high energy doesn't work (Bernstein, 2020). So instead, we have to guide ourselves gently and patiently up the scale, taking one step at a time.

As an example, let's take my thoughts from Paris and move up the emotional guidance scale:

I started at the bottom of the scale, feeling insecure, guilty, and unworthy.

My thoughts told me, "Your legs are too big."

Instead of immediately trying to jump up the scale, I would allow myself to walk through my feelings.

I asked myself, "Well, why is having big legs a bad thing?" Then I thought: "Because I worry that people won't like the way I look."

All of a sudden, I moved up the scale six places (skipping past jealousy, hatred, revenge, anger, discouragement, blame) to worry (a better-feeling emotion than insecurity).

Worry, being a higher frequency thought than insecurity, already made me feel better.

Next, I said to myself, "Well, everyone has different things they like and don't like, so it should not matter what others think about your body. What do you like about your legs?"

To which I responded, "I like that they get me places, that they are able to walk, run, and carry me up mountains. I like that they are strong."

With that, I had moved further up the scale to contentment.

There are many ways to move up the scale, leaning toward love and joy. Practicing gratitude, serving others, searching for fun, doing something you enjoy, putting the phone down, and getting outside are just a few examples. It doesn't take much. All it takes is placing your thoughts in a better place, little by little.

The next time you find yourself in a negative, low-energy place, try reaching for better-feeling thoughts and emotions.

Even just the slightest shift in your energy will help redirect you toward love and joy. As we saw in the example above, it doesn't have to be drastic. Even moving from insecurity to worry is progress.

When we feel love and joy, we give love and joy, and we attract love and joy.

PUTTING IT ALL TOGETHER

We all have bad days. We all have days when we are caught in a critical thought pattern, overthinking, and creating negative stories about ourselves and our circumstances. We all do it, probably more than we would like to admit. And it is so human! But know when you are ready to feel better, you have the power to change your thoughts. The ability to choose your labels and change your stories. The power to raise your energy. All it takes is gently reaching for those better-feeling thoughts and emotions and kindly moving yourself to a thought space with a higher vibration. It starts with tuning into your thoughts, the stories you are telling yourself, and the labels you are choosing.

WHY NOT START NOW?

Challenge #1: Find labels that feel good for you and push you forward

Earlier in the chapter, I asked you to choose labels for yourself that did not put you in a box but rather made you feel energized. Did you do it? If not, now is the time. Give yourself those uplifting labels and take away the limiting ones. Get rid of labels that put up unnecessary boundaries and ideas of who you should and shouldn't be or what you should or shouldn't do. You don't need to share these labels with anyone.

Challenge #2: Let go of the old stories

Are there any old stories you can let go of? Stories that aren't serving you or your relationships? Maybe your story is something like, "I will never be able to make that much money," or "I can't do *x*." Maybe it is, "She is just so unhelpful or ungrateful," or "He never respects what I have to say." Any story that might have been true in the past might not be true today. The stories we hold onto take up space in your life and in your relationships. The people that you hold negative biases about have probably moved on. If they moved on, you deserve to too.

We all deserve a fresh start, with the space to grow, change, learn, and mature. By getting rid of old stories and allowing people to be who they are, we will be able to see and appreciate their admirable qualities rather than being stuck on what drives you nuts. There will always be people in our lives who say and do things that we don't like or agree with, but holding onto the pain and negative energy that these people bring does not serve us. It drains us.

As for the stories you tell about yourself, you have the tools every single day, every single time you wake up, every single minute to tell yourself a new story. You might not believe your new story at first, but the more you stop yourself from opening an old book and instead start creating a new one, the closer you will get to where you want to go.

Something I have found helpful is to find a phrase, question, or word to use that disrupts your thought pattern and brings you out of the old story and into a new one.

I ask myself: "Is this story serving me?"

If it's not, write a new one.

Challenge #3: Next time you are in a low vibrational place, try and use the emotional guidance

Using the emotional guidance scale takes practice. It can be hard to self-soothe and give yourself love when you are in a low place. Everyone's ways of dealing with emotions and moving through them are different. We have to find ways that help us get to a better space.

Personally, I need space to clear my head and calm down, but after I have had my space, I seek someone comforting and express my emotions to them. For so many years, I avoided talking to people about how I felt. I just wanted to deal with my feelings on my own. But all I was really doing was pushing everything inside and, eventually, exploding. Recently, I have experienced the huge relief of talking about my feelings. I feel immediately better—or at least just lighter—talking to someone who is trustworthy. I don't intentionally use the emotional guidance scale, but as I talk and understand my emotions better, I begin to move up the scale.

The next time you are in a low place, try using the scale by asking yourself repeatedly "Why?" until you get to the root. Or, just have a conversation with someone you feel safe with about what you're going through. Even just talking it out can bring you up the scale to a higher, better-feeling emotion.

Always remember: you cannot control much in this life, but you can control your thoughts and your actions. What you think and focus on are what you create and do, and what you create and do leads you to where you are going, who you are with, and who you become. At any moment, you can change your destiny, your path, your power just by changing your thoughts, stories, and labels.

CHAPTER 14

UNLOCKING THE POWER OF YOUR MIND

———

"It's not the events that shape my life that determine how I feel and act, but rather it's the way I interpret and evaluate my life experiences. The meaning I attach to an event will determine the decisions I make, the actions I take, and therefore my ultimate destiny."

—TONY ROBBINS; AUTHOR, COACH,
INSPIRATIONAL SPEAKER

I was only twelve when my dad was diagnosed with stage three advanced Lymphoma. It was 2011, and at the time, I had never met someone who had cancer, nor did I know the gravity of the disease. I knew having cancer was bad and that many died from it, but that was the extent. I remember the day he told us like it was yesterday. It was similar to how he and my mom broke the news that we were moving to England when I was six years old. I threw a shoe at my dad's head when they told us about England. But this time, no shoes were thrown, only tears were shed.

I was happily playing with my Polly Pocket toys in my blue playroom—yes, I still played with toys at that age—when my mom called my name from downstairs. I reluctantly left my dolls behind and trudged down the stairs, eager to get back to my play. Everyone was waiting for me in the living room. My dad sat anxiously in the teal velvet armchair, my mom standing behind him, red-eyed and puffy. My brother and I sat opposite my parents on the sunken green couch. We were both unsure of what was about to be said. Would we be moving again? Did someone pass away?

My dad spoke: "I have cancer. It's called lymphoma, and it is in my spleen. I know this is scary, but I will be fine." My brother, who was fifteen and knew more than I did, asked questions, his voice shaky. My parents explained more about what this meant and how he found out, but my mind went blank. Tears filled all of our eyes as we huddled around my dad in a tight family hug. Even though I was unsure of what this all meant, we were in it together. The whole time he spoke, and in the weeks and months after, all I could think about and hope for was that *he would be fine.* I clung to his word, "I will be fine." I knew he would not lie to me. He would be fine. He *had* to be fine.

I told some friends at school about his diagnosis, and they would respond with "I am so sorry" as their faces turned to a frown, and they struggled to look me directly in the eye. Their bodies were noticeably shifting and becoming awkward. Their reactions saddened me as they were thinking about the worst-case scenario. But this wasn't going to go that way. It couldn't go that way. So I would respond, "Oh no, don't be, he is fine." And I believed myself.

I only visited him in the hospital once. My mom and I were there for his first chemo treatment—a sight I never wish on anyone. He laid in bed, hooked up to tubes, flushed and tired. Nurses came and went—chemicals pumped through his veins. Chemicals that made him feel sick and weak but would hopefully win against the growing dragon in his body. At times I had to look out the window, watching the Thames River flow and people out on the street live their lives, carefree. I couldn't bear to see someone I love in that condition, let alone my father, my hero, the rock of our family.

After that day, every chemo treatment he undertook, he did alone. He didn't want us there because he was "fine." He insisted that he was going to be *okay*. He worked out more than he did before. He ate better. He would sometimes receive chemo treatment in the morning and go straight to work afterward. He hardly took days off work. Had I not seen my dad in the hospital that first time nor watched him go completely bald, I would have never known he had cancer. He did not let his diagnosis define him or how he lived his life. He was determined to take back control.

A year later, in 2012, he was in remission. He *was* fine!

Four years later, I found out his initial "I am going to be fine" was a lie. He had stage three advanced lymphoma. It was not just in his spleen. It was also in his heart. He had a 50 percent chance of surviving. He told us he was fine because he did not want to worry us. He did not want us to know how bad it was. He wanted to be our rock even though he was the one who needed saving.

I believe a part of the reason why he beat his odds and survived was because he did not fixate on his diagnosis—he fought back. He did not pity himself or dwell on his situation. He went on living his life, working out, being more available. We were lucky he had stellar medical care in the UK, the financial means to afford it, and he was relatively young and healthy before the diagnosis. But I am confident that his outlook on his situation helped cure him. Instead of focusing on the bad and hard aspects of cancer, he focused on what was good in his life, and he did more of that. He made friends at his treatments. He kept going to work and coming home early for dinner. He hardly talked about his sickness, and instead, he took control of the aspects of his life that he had power over. He couldn't control the tumor growing and spreading inside him, but he could control his diet, his exercise, his mental state, and the story he told himself. He told himself he was going to be fine— he convinced himself just as he did us. His belief was just as crucial in curing him as the treatment he received. His story, his outlook, his actions are part of the reason he is still with us today, sitting on the couch with me as I write this.

Eight years after my dad was diagnosed and seven since he has been in remission, my mom was diagnosed with stage two lymphoma cancer, a noncurable but treatable form. Since the day she was diagnosed, my mom, too, has shown our family that no matter what life throws at us, no matter how unfair, we get to decide how much it affects us. It is about the story we tell ourselves that matters. Not every day is good. We all face hard days and hard times. It is okay to ask for help, to feel our emotions, to be human and imperfect. But all in all, our mindset, our thinking is the most powerful medicine we have.

MINDSET AS MEDICINE

Dr. Alia Crum, an assistant professor of psychology at Stanford University, has dedicated much of her professional life to studying the power of the mind. She focuses on how changes in our subjective mindsets (the assumptions we make about things) can alter our objective reality and influence our behavior, well-being, and mental and physical states. In her TEDx Talk, "Change Your Mindset, Change the Game," Dr. Crum outlines four research studies that analyze mindset and its effects on pain, exercise, diet, and stress.

The first study was performed in Italy by Dr. Benedetti and his colleagues. Dr. Benedetti studied a group of patients who had undergone thoracic heart surgery, an invasive surgery involving the organs in the chest. As routine in this surgery, patients were given a powerful painkiller called morphine to help reduce their pain. However, Dr. Benedetti made a subtle tweak. One group of patients received the morphine dosage by a doctor at their bedside, while another group received the dosage via their IV by a preprogrammed pump. Both groups received the same amount of morphine. The only difference was one group knew they were getting it, while the other did not. As it turned out, there was a difference between the two groups in their subjective pain levels. The group with morphine administered by a doctor reported significant reductions in pain levels, while the hidden morphine group didn't experience the same benefit. Their reported decrease in pain level was slower and less significant. Knowing they were receiving painkillers had a large impact on patients' pain levels, indicating a physiological influence on pain reduction.

As a division one athlete at Harvard, Dr. Crum was curious whether mindset affected the physical benefits from exercise.

In her TEDx Talk, she asked, "Was I getting fitter and stronger because of the time and the energy I was putting into my training? Or was I getting fitter and stronger because I believed I would?" Dr. Crum and Ellen Langer, a Harvard Professor, decided to test this with a group of eighty-four housekeepers working in seven different hotels across the US. Housekeepers are on their feet all day, employing a variety of different muscles and burning many calories throughout each task. Vacuuming for one burns 150–200 calories per hour. When the women were asked if they exercised regularly, two-thirds said "no." And when asked, "On a scale of zero to ten, how much exercise do you think you get?" one-third of the women replied: "zero." The women were then split into two groups and had their measurements taken: weight, blood pressure, body fat percentage, and job satisfaction. Then, Dr. Crum and Dr. Langer took one group of women and gave them a fifteen-minute presentation outlining the facts of their job and explaining to the women that their job is good exercise. They specifically mentioned that the women satisfy the General Surgeons recommended minimum of thirty minutes of exercise per day.

Four weeks later, Dr. Crum and Dr. Langer measured all the women again and found the group who didn't receive the presentation didn't change. But the group that did see the presentation lost weight, had significant reductions in blood pressure and body fat, and reported enjoying their job more. All participants assured the researchers that they had not started exercising between the initial and final measurements. While it is very plausible the women who received the presentation started working harder during their jobs, a big part of their results can be attributed to their new mindset that their work was exercise.

Dr. Crum was shocked by the results of the housekeeper study and wanted to dive deeper into whether there was a direct, immediate connection between our body and our mindset. Dr. Crum and colleagues from Yale decided to test the connection by making a big batch of milkshakes and recruiting patients to come to their lab twice and drink the milkshake. Because this was a scientific experiment and not a recipe test, patients provided blood samples and were hooked to an IV as they enjoyed the sugary beverage. The researchers wanted to study participants' ghrelin, also known as the hunger hormone. High levels of ghrelin signal to the brain that it is time to find food, while low levels suggest fullness.

The first week, participants were given a milkshake called "Sensi-Shake," which the participants were told had 140 calories, no fat, and no added sugar. They termed this "guilt-free satisfaction." After consuming the shake, researchers analyzed the participants' ghrelin response and found that there was a slight drop. Although some food was consumed, it was clearly not enough, and participants were still hungry. A week later, participants returned to the lab, and this time, they were given a milkshake, which they were told had 620 calories, fifty-six grams of sugar, and thirty grams of fat. This shake was called the "Indulgence." In response to this shake, participants' ghrelin levels dropped roughly three times more than after drinking the "Sensi-Shake." Unbeknownst to the participants, the milkshakes were the same, each time with 380 calories, forty-four grams of sugar, and thirteen grams of fat. Clearly, participants' belief that one milkshake was "indulgent" while the other was "guilt-free" played a role in their respective ghrelin levels.

The final study Dr. Crum discussed in her talk aimed to answer the question "Can our mindsets about stress influence our psychological and physiological responses?" For most individuals, stress is viewed as a negative—something bad for our health and that we want to avoid. However, a growing body of research is finding that certain amounts of stress can positively affect our well-being and performance. For this study, Dr. Crum and two Yale researchers worked with three hundred Yale employees after the 2008 financial crisis, when many worried about layoffs and paychecks. The researchers split the employees into two groups, showing one group a three-minute video about stress being debilitating and the other a video about the enhancing benefits of stress. Over the following weeks, the group who watched the "enhancing stress" video reported experiencing fewer negative health symptoms (backaches, muscle tension, insomnia) and a higher work performance and engagement. The "debilitating stress" group had negligible differences in symptoms and performance.

All four studies demonstrate that mindset plays a psychological and physiological role in determining our health, exercise, diet, and stress. This does not mean that medicine, exercise, and proper nutrition are not important in determining general wellness. But we have to start giving our mindset more credit. When we can use our mindset to our benefit, it can help change our states. As Dr. Crum states, "Mindsets can change our reality by shaping what we pay attention to, how we feel, what we do, and what our bodies prioritize and prepare to do."

Similar to the previously outlined studies, the placebo effect, in which patients who receive a placebo, a treatment, or a substance that does not provide a therapeutic effect, causes patients to report less pain and a reduction in their symptoms because of their belief that the treatment will work. Although there are no physiological benefits to the fake treatment, the mind-body connection in patients produces beneficial effects. In fact, "according to some estimates, approximately 30 percent to 60 percent of people will feel that their pain has diminished after taking a placebo pill" (Cherry, 2021). That means at least a third of all medical healing is a result of the placebo effect and the power of the mind to heal the body.

PUT YOUR PAIN ON A CLOUD

Whenever I got hurt growing up, my mom would always tell me, "Put your pain on a cloud." Truthfully, I never understood what that meant, and even to this day, it still leaves me baffled. What I do know is every time she told me that, I would picture a fluffy white cloud floating in the clear blue sky. I would then relinquish my pain to that cloud, and all of a sudden, it would burst, the remnants dusting the sky as it carried the weight of my pain. In a mere moment, for some bizarre reason that I couldn't explain, the *poof* of the cloud bursting caused my pain to *poof* as well.

Now I understand it was the power of my mind taking some of my pain away.

Our mindsets are in our control. They are our subjective interpretation of the world, an interpretation influenced by our culture, our family, our past experiences, our lifestyle. Nothing has meaning unless we give meaning to it. A long traffic light means nothing unless we decide it's going to make us late to work, and then we get angry. But that same long traffic light could also mean we have extra time to listen to our favorite music or podcast. Then suddenly, we are at peace with it. A breakup could be the worst pain you have ever felt in your life, or you could view it as a chance to work on yourself. Someone hitting your car could be a horrible and costly event, or you could make it an opportunity to reflect on how grateful you are to be able to drive and afford a car. We can reframe anything. We can choose to be a victim or a victor, angry or patient, grateful or ungrateful.

A quote that I love by Randy Pausch from *The Last Lecture* is: "You can't change the cards you're dealt with, but you can change how you play them." We cannot control the external events that happen in our life. But we can control how we view the events. We can control our opinion—whether we view them as good or bad, fair or unfair. We can control our actions. And most of the time, it's not what happens to you that determines your fate. It's how you interpret the situation and the actions you take. You get to decide how you want to feel, who you want to be, how you want to act and react. It all starts in the mind, and your mind is in your control.

. . .

"Accept then act. Accept what is as though you have chosen it. Always work with it, not against it."

—Eckhart Tolle

. . .

HOW TO USE THE POWER OF MINDSET TO YOUR ADVANTAGE:

1. You can't control what happens, but you can control how you react

As Eckart Tolle, a spiritual teacher and best-selling author, says, "Accept what is as though you have chosen it." I know there are thousands of circumstances we all face that we would never wish upon our worst enemies. In our challenges, we need to feel our feelings, sit and move through the pain. Feeling your feelings is incredibly important in any healing and growing process. But dwelling on our situations and wasting energy wishing they could change does not move us forward. We have to shift our perspective and move toward accepting our reality before we can gain the clarity we need to guide our actions toward a better place. We have to use our energy and power to work with our realities rather than against them. We cannot move forward and make things better if we are stuck in the yuck of it all.

Accept your situation as if you wanted it and take action from there.

2. View setbacks and challenges as opportunities for growth

Remember when you were a child, and you thought your parents knew everything? Then you got older and realized everyone is human. Life is meant for living and learning. It is impossible to sail through life without setbacks and "failures." Every blip and bump in the road teaches us something. Each bump causes us to slow down for a minute to take in our surroundings and make sure we are going in the right direction. Each blip makes us more cautious and better able to handle hard things. Blips teach us that we are not invincible and remind us how blessed we are. If we take the bumps and blips as opportunities to learn and grow, we will be better off.

3. ACT

Acknowledge, Change, Thrive.

Whenever you notice your mindset and thoughts drifting toward the negative, acknowledge the thought. Ask yourself, is this thought serving me? Am I in control of this situation?

If it is out of your control and the thought is not serving you, change the thought to something more productive and more helpful. If the situation is in your control, what can you change to make it better? What action will lead you to where you want to go? Once you have changed the thought or your actions, go out and thrive.

For example, let's say you arrange a party with friends. At the last minute, a few of your friends text you saying they can't make it. You feel sad and frustrated because you spent a lot of time preparing for the party and you were excited to see everyone. Your thoughts jump to: "I am so mad at them, they knew how much this meant, this party is going to be bad," or "I can't believe they did this to me." Since you notice your thoughts and mindset become focused on the negative, take a step back and acknowledge them. Ask yourself, "Can I control what my friends do or say?" No. "Is getting down about this serving me?" No. "What can I do to change?" You can't control anyone in this situation but yourself, but you can start by changing your mindset. So you might think, "I have a lot of other friends who are coming I am so excited to see! Even though I am sad some friends are no longer coming, I am still looking forward to the evening." You have acknowledged the thought and changed it, and now you are in a better place to enjoy your time!

My dad often uses the phrase "Don't auto-piss yourself off." I never really thought too much about what it meant until a few years ago. I think what he meant was just this kind of thing: don't spin stories in your head that make you unhappy.

CHAPTER 15

YOUR INTUITION HAS YOUR BACK

————

"My intuition never fails me. It is I who fail when I do not listen to it."

—HAZRAT INAYAT KHAN; SUFI TEACHER

A bagel can mean many things to different people—a delicious carb, a typical morning breakfast, a cherished Sunday ritual, the only way to breakfast for Yom Kippur. But to me, in this story, a bagel means repairing an awkward tension in a friendship.

You see, when you live in a twelve-foot by ten-foot dorm room with your bed only a few feet away from your roommate's, there is bound to be some tension. This was especially true during my junior year of college. My roommate of three years and good friend, Grace, and I were both in the midst of a stressful semester. We were both planning on studying abroad in the spring, and I had just embarked on my first complete semester in business school. We were drowning in work during midterms and had mixed emotions about spending a semester away from school, and for me, my then-boyfriend. Two girls, one small room, heavy internal emotions can quickly lead to a fizzle. We ended up getting off on the wrong foot at a point. The energy in our shared room was thick with negativity. We barely spoke to each other. Only a handful of "hellos" were shared when we crossed paths. Not out finest rooming moment.

A few days into the weirdness, I was walking back to school from a workout class off-campus. On my way back, I passed by her favorite bagel store. I usually glance in the window to admire the decor and people watch, but that day, I felt compelled to enter. Without a second thought, my gut intuition had flung open the door, jostling the bells to welcome me as I stood at the counter, ordering her favorite bagel. Moments later, I was on my way back, a lightly toasted everything bagel with cream cheese in tow.

Back in the room, Grace was sitting huddled over her desk as she prepared for a quiz later in the week. She offered a chilly "Hi" when I entered, not bothering to look up from her work. *Yup, still tension,* I thought as I walked over to where she was and handed her the bag of heaven in bread form. Her eyes shot from the bag to me, then back to the bag, the thick air of tension surrounding us evaporating immediately.

You would have thought I gave this girl my kidney by her reaction. Grace was surprised, delighted, and grateful. She turned her chair around as I sat down in mine. We talked for an hour, discussing life and our past weeks as if nothing had ever felt off between us. All the negative energy, awkwardness, and uncomfortable tensions were healed by a bagel. Oh, the amazing things carbs can do for us!

LET YOUR GUT GUIDE YOU

I did not consciously decide to get that bagel. I walk past the shop every day and have never once stepped in. My gut took over and told me, "This bagel, one of the greatest carbs, this is the perfect peace offering." My gut intuition solved the weirdness.

I know this isn't some miraculous story of how my intuition spoke to me and led me to save lives or become a millionaire, but maybe today it didn't, and tomorrow it does! The point is that we all have an inner voice that is wise and well-meaning. This intuition, gut feeling, knowing, inner voice, whatever you want to call it, reveals who we are at our core and the knowledge we have from previous experiences. It allows us to act quickly and confidently without the need for decision-making or logic. You don't need to consult someone else, spend hours debating, or make a pro and con list. You just know. This all-knowing feeling is there to help guide you to your next destination.

Our knowing or intuition is not random. It is a product of automatic brain processing that rapidly sifts through and pattern matches your current experience to past experiences and knowledge. Your intuition presents a swift decision based on what is stored in your long-term memory ("Intuition," 2021). The feeling and knowing it provides comes from a deep part of us and creates a level of awareness that you can trust with emotional certainty.

Although there is not abundant scientific data on the topic, one study conducted by a team of researchers from the University of New South Wales has been able to prove intuition does exist. Researchers designed an experiment in which a group of twenty college students were shown moving black-and-white dots on one half of a computer screen. The dots looked like noise on an old TV. Students were asked to decide which way the dots were moving, either to the left or to the right. As participants were asked to make this decision, on the other half of the computer screen, they saw a bright, flashing square of color. Occasionally this colorful square was embedded with an image designed to trigger an emotional response. In order to elicit a positive emotion, participants saw a picture of a puppy or baby, and in order to elicit a negative emotion, they saw a picture of a gun or snake. However, the participants were unaware of these images because they flashed too quickly to register. The quick flashes of images were meant to simulate the type of information involved in intuition—quick, tied to emotions, and subconsciously perceived.

Across four different experiments, the researchers found that participants were able to make faster and more accurate decisions when they unconsciously viewed the emotional images (Nierenberg, 2016). Individuals' brains were able to use the images to improve their decision-making. The lead author of the study and associate professor of psychology, Joel Pearson, noted that, "Another interesting finding in this study is that intuition improved over time, suggesting that the mechanisms of intuition can be improved with practice" (Lufityanto et al., 2016). Ultimately, the studied proved that information subconsciously absorbed by the brain will help make decisions faster and more accurate if the information holds value beyond what is already registered in the conscious mind.

Albert Einstein was once quoted saying, "The intuitive mind is a sacred gift and the rational mind is a faithful servant. We have created a society that honors the servant and has forgotten the gift." Albert Einstein, one of the most intelligent minds and the father of the theory of relativity, believed in the power of intuition.

Listen to your gut, your intuition, and follow those impulse decisions. It is something higher than you—a higher being or your higher self—that is speaking through you, telling you what your next move needs to be. This feeling is meant to bring more abundance and positivity into your life. This feeling is a push in the right direction. Whenever I feel intuition speaking through me, I smile and act on it—I know it is leading me to where I should be.

IT LEADS YOU WHERE YOU NEED TO GO

The solar eclipse (which occurs on average every 375 years) happened during the first week of my freshman year of college. Everyone was eager to go outside, stare at the sky, and watch the magic happen. Some even made makeshift cardboard telescopes. And by some people, I mean my mom, and she was *really* proud of hers.

A few days into my first week of college, I was alone in my dorm room, hanging up pictures on my wall, when I got a text from my mom that the eclipse would be happening soon, followed by a picture of her telescope creation. I didn't have any solid friends at that point, so I decided I would just walk to the quad and see it by myself. As I descended the steps and started walking out of my residence hall, I got an impulse to go back inside and walk down the corridor to see if anyone wanted to join.

This is very unlike me. I am a wholehearted introvert, not one to be bold and ask someone to hang out. But I couldn't ignore this feeling. I swiftly turned around, walked back up to my floor, and down the hall to see if anyone had their door open.

Out of the twenty dorm rooms on my hall, there was one door open, a few rooms down from mine. After I took a deep breath, I stopped at the open doorway and peered my head in. Two girls sat at their desks and turned to me. Their faces were soft and kind, with a small smile hinting that I was a pleasant surprise. "Hey! I am Livia, I was going to go watch the eclipse, and I was wondering if you guys wanted to join!" Their smiles grew as they introduced themselves and followed me out to the quad. Their names were Emma and Katie.

After watching the eclipse and getting to know each other more, Emma and I decided to walk around campus, mostly eager to explore "Eagle Row," where all the fraternity and sorority houses were. Emma and I laughed, talked about our plans for college, our hometowns, and high schools. I immediately liked her and felt like I had made my first college friend.

Not only was Emma my first college friend, but she is one of my closest friends to this day. My college experience would not have been the same without her—from hours studying in the library, to our long daily walks, to traveling abroad together. She is the much-needed voice of reason and spontaneous fun that I wanted in my life.

Who knows whether we would have been friends had I not had that impulse (intuition) to go back inside and find an open door. Her open door.

. . .

*"Trust your instincts. It's the universe inspiring you,
speaking to you. It's the universe communicating with you
on the receiving frequency."*

—Rhonda Byrne, The Secret

. . .

CONNECTING TO YOUR INNER KNOWING

If you are willing to sit alone with your thoughts, sit in the quiet stillness of your being, you will know what to do. Your thoughts, especially your subconscious, are your best guides.

My grandma is a therapist and helped write a book on intuition. When talking to my grandma about this topic, she told me, "Intuition is a real skill, available to everyone. What usually gets in the way is our very active interest in logic and linear thinking. Because intuition is often not provable, we tend to discount it. Logic comes to a provable conclusion, so we tend to value it more."

But even though intuition, our knowing, isn't necessarily logical or explained by science, that doesn't mean you shouldn't trust it. It is speaking to you for a reason.

In her best-selling memoir, *Untamed,* Glennon Doyle frequently writes about her knowing and how it has played an important part in her adult life. Glennon describes how she started working toward finding her knowing by sitting in her closet, on a towel, door locked, eyes closed, just breathing. At first, this felt unnatural, and her mind wandered as she thought of the other hundred things she could be doing instead of sitting in a closet. But after a few weeks of practice, like someone working on stretching, she was able to go lower and deeper within herself during each closet attendance. Each session, she learned to go inward, deep down to the quiet stillness, and connect to her gut knowing.

Glennon's practice sounds like meditation, but that is because yoga, breathwork, meditation, anything that gets you to calm your busy mind, helps us tap into our intuition.

In *Untamed*, Glennon writes, "Down here, when I pose a question about my life—in words or abstract images—I sense a nudge... the knowing would meet me in the deep and nudge me toward the next right thing, one thing at a time. That was how I began to know what to do next. That was how I began to walk through my life more clearly, solidly, and steady."

Everyone's knowing is different. But as Glennon said, it is a nudge deep within us that when we practice mindfulness and get to a quiet stillness, we will find an inner voice that has the answer.

HOW TO FIND THE KNOWING

To find the knowing takes practice and mindfulness. It takes pausing and stepping back in a moment of uncertainty to connect with yourself and see if you find yourself pushed in a certain direction.

Steps to help you find the knowing:

- Uncertainty and questioning arises
- Stop and step back
    - Instead of looking to external sources for the answer: friends, social media, or Google; step back, look within, and ask yourself for the answer.

- Focus on your breath
  - Take time to consciously breathe. Breathing helps us center ourselves and better connect with our being.
  - A breathing technique I like for calming the mind is the four-seven-eight exercise. In this method, you inhale for a count of four, hold your breath for a count of seven, and exhale for a count of eight, repeating the exercise until you feel more relaxed.
- Connect to yourself and to your feelings
  - Dig deep within. The answers to many of your questions may be hidden in your unconscious mind.
- Feel around for the knowing
  - Sit still, practice mindfulness, and see if you feel a push toward a certain thought or action.
- Follow the direction it is pushing you toward
- Don't question, don't explain, just do
- Let it be what it is
  - Trust the knowing. It is there for a reason! Our knowing often knows best.
- Repeat whenever another moment of uncertainty arises
  - Keep trusting your gut and practice tuning into the knowing. Like any skill, it gets better the more you practice it.

Intuition is personal, and thus how we sense the knowing may differ between one another. When I asked my grandma how you feel your intuition, she said, "It often comes to you differently than thoughts. For some, it comes in word form, others see pictures, and some have sensations or feelings." For me, it is an impulse to act. Before I am even consciously aware of what I am doing, I am acting on the feeling.

Obviously, there are times where it is wiser to use intuition and times when it is not. Decisions that require experts, have objective criteria, clear rules, and ample amounts of data (such as doctors making medical diagnoses) should not be based on intuition (Locke, 2020). However, most decisions lie in the gray area between intuitive judgment and data. When buying a car, individuals rely on information about gas mileage, features, and safety ratings, but they also use their own guide to decide if they like the look and feel of the car. They use available information, but the ultimate decision may largely be influenced by their feelings. Where intuition is usually the most helpful is when quick decisions must be made and very little information is needed to make the decision.

The way to learn about how we sense our knowing is to get to know it, to connect with it through mindfulness and presence—through being aware of our bodies, our thoughts, our energies. Glennon did this through a closet session. Some do it through yoga, meditation, journaling, daily nature walks. Find what works for you.

ALLOW YOUR INNER WORLD TO TRANSFORM YOUR OUTER WORLD

If it cannot be proven by ample amounts of scientific data, the proof of intuition lies in individuals' collective experiences with it. If you search on Google "intuition stories," you will be met with hundreds, if not thousands of stories where someone's intuition got them out of a bad situation, put them in the right place at the right time, or saved a life. The stories speak for themselves. In moments of loss, uncertainty, or feelings of unease, tune into your body, your mind, and connect with your being. It might just lead you exactly where you need to go.

· · ·

"When we let ourselves feel, our inner self transforms. When we act upon our knowing and imagination, our outer worlds transform. Living from the worlds within us will change our outer worlds."

—Glennon Doyle, Untamed

· · ·

Some people believe intuition is the universe speaking to us. Others believe it is just woo-woo. Whatever your stance may be, there is nothing bad that can come from learning to become more attuned to your thoughts and body. Many entrepreneurs and highly successful people heavily rely on their gut feelings when making decisions. Steve Jobs, CEO and cofounder of Apple Inc., is one of many accomplished individuals who are big proponents of intuition. In an interview with *The New York Times*, Jobs said, "Intuition is a very powerful thing, more powerful than intellect, in my opinion. That's had a big impact on my work" (Isaacson, 2011).

His work led him to create and run one of the most successful businesses in the world.

Obviously, intuition is not solely responsible for Job's success, but there is something to say that one of the most influential entrepreneurs believed intuition is more powerful than intellect.

No matter who you are or what you believe, we all have access to the power of our intuition and the level of awareness it provides. All we have to do is take the time to ground ourselves, breathe, and listen to the voice deep within us. We often know the answer. It is within us, hidden in our unconscious, waiting for you to sink deep and find it.

Start connecting with your knowing. Who knows what messages are waiting to be heard?

CHAPTER 16

LEAVE WHAT DOESN'T SERVE YOU

———

"When we can let go of what other people think and own our story, we gain access to our worthiness, the feeling that we are enough just as we are and that we are worthy of love and belonging."

—BRENÉ BROWN; RESEARCHER AND AUTHOR

We've all set out to organize our closets at least once in our lives just to find our vision blurred with all sorts of colors. It seems like a daunting task at first, but it becomes cathartic for the soul once you start developing a rhythm. This is what I found myself in the middle of one day as I opened my closet with a plastic bag in hand, ready to let go.

I take the first jumpsuit off the hanger. It is striped cream and beige with ruffle sleeves and a belt that ties in the front. I loved it when I got it two years ago, but I have outgrown it, so in the bag it goes off to a better home. The next piece I pull is my prom dress, a long figure-hugging red dress. A dress that once made me feel the most on top of the world I have ever felt.

Although I wore it five years ago and do not have an occasion to wear it to now, I put it back in its rightful place between my other favorite dresses, knowing that one day I might have an opportunity to wear it again or even loan it to a friend.

I continue going through my wardrobe until the donation bag is full to the brim, and what is left hanging in my closet are clothes that fit me and fit where I am in life. Keeping things that, as tidying expert Marie Kondo would say, "spark joy."

My space has suddenly grown without the clutter. I freed up space that new items can fill or space where emptiness makes me feel calmer.

Which has me thinking...

What if we did this with other aspects of our lives? What if we let go of things we have outgrown, things that no longer serve us or hold us back?

What if we let go of that toxic ex? That friend that always makes us feel badly about ourselves? That bad habit?

We have to Marie Kondo our lives, not just our belongings— although that is good too and incredibly therapeutic. Going through our mental baggage and asking: "Does this person, idea, belief, action, behavior, feeling serve me or is it causing me to think negatively? Is it preventing me from becoming who I want to be? Does it resonate with my ideal self?"

Whatever it is, if it's not serving you, can you release it?

The funny thing about letting go is the decision to do it, and the moments before feel hard, scary, and uncertain. However, as soon as you release whatever is holding you back, you will feel a sense of relief. Think of it like having training wheels on a bike when you were young. You used the training wheels to learn how to ride but after a while, you no longer need them. It might be scary to take them off. You might not think you are ready. But when you finally get them off and realize you can bike on your own, you get excited about all the things you can do and explore.

Over time, this can feel like freedom.

I know from experience that the times I have let go, whether it was of a person or a way of thinking, I have gained so much.

CREATING SPACE FOR BETTER TO COME

In college, I started seeing a guy three months before the summer. We hit it off immediately. Soon, we started spending a lot of time together, texting all day, sneaking glances in class, studying for hours in the library when neither of us had that much work. After only three weeks of talking, I went with him to his fraternity formal—a weekend that cemented my strong feelings for him. I was trying to play things cool, so I never asked to define what we were. In my mind, we were heading for a relationship title, and I got that vibe from him too.

The excitement died down when a week after we got back from formal; I saw his ex's name pop up on his phone every time we hung out. He and his ex had only broken up a few months prior. I wanted to give him the benefit of the doubt, to believe he was just trying to be friends with her. So, I did. I didn't ask about it until one day we were driving in his car when she started FaceTiming him. Before the second ring, he quickly declined the call, clearly trying to hide it from me. We both knew I saw it. I innocently asked, "Oh, are you guys still talking?" To which he nervously replied, "Um yeah, yeah, we are. We dated for a while and were best friends growing up, so we are trying to be friends."

I desperately wanted that to be true, so I took his comment at face value.

With the ambiguity of what we were, his past relationship, and his flirty demeanor, my head and my heart were in a constant conflict. My heart wanted to be with him, but my head sent out multiple red warning signals. For months all I could talk about was him. I analyzed every text, every time we hung out, every glance or lack thereof. My friends and my mom were sick of hearing about him. And frankly, I was sick of talking about him. It even got to the point that my phone would autocorrect different words to his name because I talked about him that much!

When the summer was only a few weeks away, we finally talked and defined what we were. We both wanted something with each other but decided it was not the right time for labels. Well... he decided it was not the right time for labels. He expressed to me there was no one else he wanted to be with, a feeling I returned. In the end, we agreed to keep talking and pick things up in the fall.

Two weeks into the summer, I found out he was still seeing his ex and had even gone to visit her when we left school. I didn't want to let go because I had created this story in my head of all the things we could be if he could just be the person I wanted him to be. I didn't want to let go of that dream and the comfort of being with someone. But after a two-hour *mature* conversation on text...

I finally ended things.

For three months, I spent all my mental energy on him and school. Now with both over, I had so much free space and energy that I could devote to myself.

That was the summer I trained for the half marathon, worked at my dream internship, and worked as a waitress. That summer was one of the happiest times of my life. I was free to spend my time on things that made me feel good and gave me energy. At work, I was completely myself. I made friends, met my mentors, and figured out what I wanted in life and who I wanted to be.

That spring, a few months prior, I was dwelling over mixed signals. I received reassuring cute text messages, but hours later, I caught a glimpse of his phone lighting up with Tinder notifications and other girls' messages. I wouldn't make plans with friends on the slight chance I would get a last-minute text from him asking to hang out. I paid more attention to his needs and wants than my own.

As it would also turn out, a week after I ended things with that guy, I met a coworker who happened to be going to my college in the fall. A coworker turned friend and eventually boyfriend.

When we let go of the people not fueling us, we create space for better people and experiences to enter our lives.

Every time I have ended a toxic relationship, I have attracted great people in my life, whether they are friends, coworkers, mentors, or romantic partners.

You only have so much mental space and energy, only so much time to spend doing things. Spend time with the ones you care about and spend your energy on the things that fuel you.

"LETTING GO CAN MAKE YOU UNSTOPPABLE"

Those are the words Jill Sherer Murrey used to open up her TEDxTalk titled "The Unstoppable Power of Letting Go," words that Jill herself has experienced to be true.

At forty-one years old, the death of a relationship showed Jill "how to truly let go of what wasn't working."

For forty-one years, Jill lived her life solely in the present, not thinking about the future. Or, as Jill likes to say, "I kind of lived my life like a dog—moment to moment—I chased balls, I ate whatever I could off the ground."

Jill felt like she had it all. She had great friends, a great job, a great actual dog, and a great boyfriend named Hector.

A boyfriend of twelve years whom she loved dearly, who treated her well and had many great characteristics but who could not commit to her. Jill would say, "I want to get married."

Hector would reply, "Not yet." When Jill suggested living together, Hector responded, "Not yet."

"Not yet" was Hector's favorite catchphrase but to Jill, "Not yet was a bad song I could not get out of my head."

The more "not yet" Jill heard, the more she just thought it was just a "not now." But twelve years later, "not yet" had suddenly felt like "not ever."

So, after twelve years, Jill finally decided to let go, but not just of Hector. Jill said, "I had to let go of Hector and of the idea of marrying him or anybody. Because at forty-one, my options were scary."

Jill had to let go of her fear of losing Hector, "The fear that [she] would grow old and die alone, that [her] friends would use [her] as a cautionary tale, that it was too late for [her]."

But despite all her fears, Jill had to finally admit to herself what she really wanted, and what she wanted was to have more.

When the reality of her situation and her desires for more set in, Jill made a plan. A plan that, as she thought through each step, became clearer and made her feel more certain. Her plan was to quit her job, sell her condo, and hug her friends goodbye.

A plan to let go of everything, to start fresh, and to start a new life in New Hope, Pennsylvania. The irony that she moved to a town called "New Hope" is not lost on me.

Although it was hard to let everything go, to let Hector go, Jill knew she needed the fresh start, and within a year of living in New Hope, Jill met her husband, Daniel.

Unfortunately, when Jill was fifty years old, Hector died of cancer. Through her grief, Jill clung to the promise she made to herself at forty-one, the promise, "that I would never take time for granted again. Instead, I would use it to let go, to create space for the things I really wanted and for what mattered most."

A promise she would make each day special and create a life she was proud of.

Through her journey, Jill learned five key ways to let go. Five ideas that have not only helped her let go in the past but let go of what is holding her back each and every day.

1. Let go of taking things personally: "If people aren't giving you what you want, or if they're just behaving badly. Most of the time that is their problem, not yours."

2. Let go of what other people think: "There is a rule in business that states: whenever you are putting something out there. Ten percent of people will hate it. Eighty percent of people will be indifferent, and 10 percent will be your raving fan."

3. Let go of trying to be something you are not: "There are some things we just can't change about ourselves, and that's a good thing."

4. Let go of the need to be perfect: "Who wants to be friends with someone who is perfect? Think about that."

5. Let go of not yet: "If there is something you want to do, make a plan and act, but don't wait."

Each day Jill uses these five ideas and the reminder that "It's the phone call I can't make that reminds me to make every day count. And I encourage you all to do the same. Whatever that is, I say, let go for it."

LET IT GO:

Here is a quick exercise for you. Get a pen and paper or just sit in a comfortable, quiet space and think. In all aspects of your life, what do you need to let go of? Is it negative self-talk? Maybe an unhealthy habit like drinking too much soda or ordering delivery every night. Could it be spending too much time on social media? Take a few moments to sit with this question. What are you holding onto in your life that is holding you back?

Once you have that list, because I know we all have at least one thing, what are some steps you can start doing to help you let go and move forward? Would seeing a therapist help? Maybe starting a habit of journaling or meditating every night? How about joining a support group or a group activity you always wanted to do?

How can you move forward from here, clear the space, and become freer?

Here are some things I personally need to let go of that I am sure many of you may relate to.

LET GO OF THE NEED TO BE AND LOOK PERFECT

Our lives were never supposed to be cookie-cutter and perfect. We are supposed to look different, to be different. For most of us, at the end of the day, our goal is to just be happy. Chasing perfectionism only leads us to a less happy place. The way to find happiness and fulfillment is by learning to love who we are.

Plus, usually, the happiest people are the prettiest people. I can still remember people from my childhood just because they were always so happy!

LET GO OF COMPARISONS

As Iyanla Vanzant once said, "Comparison is an act of violence against the self." I am no stranger to comparison. All day, whether it is on my phone, my computer, or in real life, I compare myself to others. Not just my looks, but my achievements, my style, my work ethic. And let me tell you, it is exhausting and hard to stop! What I have learned is to just be happy for the people I see, to give them silent praise, and then return that to myself. We will always want what we don't have, but if we spend our time wishing we had more, we forget all that we do have.

You might not know it, but there are tons of people sending silent praises to you.

LET GO OF BEING YOUR OWN WORST CRITIC

Let's face it, most of us are our own worst critics. I know I am. A lot of times, our self-criticism is about things we don't notice in other people or things about us no one else would notice. What if we turned things around and all started treating ourselves like we would our friends? Be your own hype woman or man. Nothing bad would come from having a little more confidence in ourselves.

LET GO OF THE NEED TO CONTROL EVERYTHING

The only thing we will ever have control over is ourselves. When we let go of the need to control, we can relax and just embrace what is as though we asked for it. Life is so unpredictable. Just look at the 2020 pandemic! We cannot know where it will take us or what will come up. If we hold onto the need to control everything or everyone, chances are, we will be let down. The only thing you can ever fully control is your thoughts, your actions, and the story you tell yourself.

LET GO OF THE PEOPLE WHO BRING YOU DOWN

The people you spend the most time with will have the biggest impact on who you become. Whether you are aware of it or not, they have the power to shape you. As motivational speaker Jim Rohn put it: "You are the average of the five people you spend the most time with." Make sure the people you surround yourself with are people who will have a positive impact on you.

LET GO OF WHAT OTHER PEOPLE THINK

What others think or say says more about them than about you. We see in others what we don't like about ourselves.

Anything negative someone has to say about you is a reflection of their own wounds.

LET GO OF HIDING BEHIND A FACADE

In her book *The Gifts of Imperfection,* author Brené Brown writes, "Owning our story can be hard but not nearly as difficult as spending our lives running from it." By accepting who we are and living as that person, we attract people who love us for us. I would rather be surrounded by people who love me as I am than people who love me as they think I am.

LET GO OF PAST HURTS

Try and use your past experiences as wisdom, not wounds. Learn from what happened, use it to help guide you in similar situations, let it make you grow. Don't forget the past; it is a powerful teacher that can redirect you to better ways of being. But the past is behind us. It cannot be recreated or changed. It is gone, and by constantly looking in the rearview mirror, you are missing what's going on in front and around you. Don't miss out on living in the now because you are living in the past.

LET GO OF LIVING IN THE FUTURE

As my great-grandmother used to say, "Don't wish your days away." Just like what happens if we live in the past, if we live in the future, we are missing out on the now. The future is shaped by the now, so if we aren't consciously present, we aren't consciously taking part in shaping our future. When we look toward something that is not here yet, we miss out on enjoying the present and seeing all there is to see. We might not even recognize new opportunities that are right in front of us. Moments cannot be recreated. Everything happens only once. Enjoy the time you have when you have it.

LET GO OF NEGATIVE SELF-TALK

Our thoughts impact our realities. They shape who we are and how we see the world. When we think negatively, we attract more of it into our life. When we change the thoughts we have to be more in line with who we want to be and how we want to feel and act, we begin to attract what we want.

LET GO OF NEEDING OTHERS APPROVAL

When we live from the outside in, we are letting other people's opinions affect how we live our lives. When we start to live from the inside out, we let our own awareness guide us. What others think or say about you does not define who you are. You are only defined by what you think of yourself.

LET GO OF SELF-JUDGMENT

When we appreciate all we are, we won't accept less than we deserve.

LET GO OF BEING ANYONE BUT YOU

It's a shame to waste your life running away from the person that you are or spending your life pursuing someone else's life.

Letting go starts with reflection. With recognizing what it is that is taking up space, energy, time. Once we realize the things, thoughts, people, actions that are cluttering our spaces, we can start the process of tidying up. We want our spaces, our literal and mental spaces, to fill with things that "spark joy."

Let's all start letting go of the things in our lives that don't serve us, that don't spark joy.

. . .

"In the end, only three things matter: how much you loved, how gently you lived, and how gracefully you let go of things not meant for you."

—Gautama Buddha

. . .

PART FIVE:

LASTING

CHAPTER 17

THE POWER OF RITUALS

———

"You will never change your life until you change something you do daily. The secret of your success is found in your daily routine."

—JOHN C. MAXWELL; AUTHOR

I wake up at seven every morning. Sometimes this can be 6:30 a.m. or 7:30 a.m., depending on how crazy I feel that day. Nevertheless, most days, including weekends, I roll over at seven and switch off the *rather* obnoxious melody streaming from my phone. I then open the clock app and turn off the other two alarms that will go off in five and ten minutes, respectively. My anxiety insists on setting three alarms in the off chance I do not wake up for the first.

Once I am up, I make my bed and go to the bathroom to do my bathroom morning routine; brush my teeth, wash my face, you know the deal. Back in my room, I climb out of my PJs and opt for the workout clothes that my last night self left for me to wear today. Once my leggings have been pulled to my waist and the struggle to get my sports bra on is accomplished, I lace up my shoes and head out the door for my morning walk.

Depending on the day—and the company—this can be any-where from a two-mile walk to a six-mile walk. If I am back at school with my good friend Emma, this means six-mile walks every morning, even if it's cold and dark out. We gossip our way into the day and wake ourselves up walking the same few loops. If this is over a school break when I walk with my mom, this means two miles if she has it her way or four miles if I have it my way.

I enjoy the walk, but near the end, I am mentally getting ready for the next part of my day, my mind moving to the next tick to cross off my list. Once home, I run to my spin bike and log onto my virtual class. I bought an at-home spin bike at the beginning of May 2020, and it has been my saving grace. I dance, sweat, and climb hills, all while going nowhere for forty-five minutes. It is a blast and gets my endorphins fired up. By the end of the class, my legs can no longer move, and I feel excited and ready for a productive day! I pull myself from the bike and hop in the shower.

In the shower, I plan the rest of my day in my head and dream of the breakfast I am going to make. I eat the same breakfast every morning, the same variation of oatmeal and coffee. I make my breakfast in my calculated way: boil, pour, stir, ber-ries, mix, pour, add toppings, and then I sit down and enjoy my breakfast in peace. Thirty minutes later, the coffee hits, and work mode has officially begun. I sit down at my desk, pry my laptop open, and begin the next few tasks of the day. I get to work.

Every day is the same. My routine does change from time to time, especially when I am in a new season of life, but 90 percent of the time, it is the same thing, day in and day out, weekends included.

My routine is extreme, but it works for me! I feel productive, energized, and balanced—I always make sure I have time to spend doing things I love and being with the people I love.

Another person may sleep until 8 a.m., do their espresso ritual, and read a book for an hour.

Someone else may roll out of bed five minutes before they have to be out the door for work, work all day, come home, and watch television until bed.

Every routine can be completely different. The important part is the structure, not the actual tasks you complete.

If a routine works for you, fuels you, and gives you energy, then keep on keeping on!

THE BENEFITS OF ROUTINES

Routines don't just help us get tasks done. They are highly beneficial for our physical and mental health.

Research on the benefits of routines has consistently shown routines help improve mental health, especially when it comes to managing stress and anxiety (Cherry, 2020). Individuals with solid routines report lower stress levels and increased productivity. Routines have also been found to improve sleep and energy levels. Creating a consistent sleep schedule of going to bed and waking up around the same time results in more alertness, better immune function, less irritability, sharper focus, and short-term memory (Peters, 2020). A routine sleep schedule can help you have more natural energy through-out the day, so you won't need to keep running to the coffee maker! These benefits are often not drastic changes that you can see overnight. They're small changes that, over time, will contribute to your overall well-being.

Routines keep things in line and expected. They offer a treasured comforting regularity in a world of unknowns. They can improve our stress levels, mood, sleep, well-being, connections, among many more. Depending on the routine you establish, certain parts of your hectic day are already controlled for and taken care of. You take out the guesswork of "When should I work out?" or "When do I have time to do this chore?" Routines give your day structure. You know when to do each task and the time allotted to work on it. You won't need to constantly do catch-up on your tasks from the day before or expend mental energy worrying when you will get things done. It is already planned and accounted for; all you need to do is get busy.

Routines are also a part of self-care. They allow you to create direction for your day, so you can carve out time to focus on your needs. I make my mornings and my evenings about me, and the rest of my day is devoted to work and productivity. My mornings are for moving and grounding myself. I set myself up for an energizing day through a movement-filled morning, and I ground myself through my walks and peaceful breakfasts. My nights are for winding down. I focus intently on my skincare (which I find therapeutic), and I make sure to watch something lighthearted before bed. I want to make sure I go to bed anxiety-free and spend my evenings surrounded by joy. At times, usually when I am most on my game, I opt to read before bed, and I start my mornings with journaling and gratitude. These activities increase my mood for the day and calm my brain before bed.

Think about your goals. What do you want to accomplish in a day? What do you need more of? What are your hobbies? It is important to make time for the things you enjoy doing.

Grinding all the time will just lead to burnout and high-stress levels. Creating a balanced routine is the key to getting things done *while* enjoying life. Focus on what you want to add to your life and start establishing routines around that. Want more time to read? Devote time in your day to reading. Want to start eating better? Plan time in your week to meal prepping, cooking, and grocery shopping. Plan for success, and you will be more successful. The more tasks can cross off in a day, the more wins you will have, the more confident you will be, the more at peace you will feel. Win, win, win, win!

EVERYONE'S ROUTINES ARE DIFFERENT

Do you want to know who likes to win too? Pretty much every single successful person you admire. I think you would be hard-pressed to find one well-known individual who does not have a special routine or ritual they follow each day.

Tony Robbins, motivational speaker and a self-development guru, starts each day plunging into a pool of 57°F (13°C) water. What is Mr. Robbins "why" around this? Robbins says: "I do it because there is nothing that can change everything in your system like a radical change in temperature. Every organ, every nerve in your body is on fire" (Roomer, 2019).

Dramatic? Yes. Would I ever do it? Nope. Does it work for him? Absolutely. It gets him ready for the day by shocking his body first thing. His "why" is to start the day disciplined and ready for whatever comes at him.

Arianna Huffington, cofounder of the Huffington Post, says, "A big part of my morning ritual is about what I don't do: when I wake up, I don't start the day by looking at my smartphone. Instead, once I'm awake, I take a minute to breathe deeply, be grateful, and set my intention for the day." (Huffington, 2021). Huffington starts her day social media free and full of gratitude, something I have been trying to do but having a hard time with. Nonetheless, I aspire to successfully incorporate this into my routine someday.

Steve Jobs, cofounder of Apple Inc., started each day reminding himself of his dreams. In a speech to Stanford graduates, Jobs told the crowd that every morning he asks himself the same question: "If today was the last day of my life, would I want to do what I'm doing today?" (Adams, 2017). For Jobs, this question allowed him to make sure he was implementing the right changes in his life to conquer his dreams. Jobs always focused on living his life fully.

FIND WHAT WORKS FOR YOU

We all have routines, whether we know it or not. That includes the way we make the bed every morning, go to church every Sunday, attend a weekly fitness class, or celebrate holidays the same way every year. We are all creatures of routine in one way or another.

Take a step back and look at the things you routinely do. Is this routine increasing your productivity? Does it ground you and give you energy? Is it healthy for your mind and body? Do you dedicate time to your relationships in your routine?

Taking time to reflect on your current behaviors could help you see where you need to add in more time for yourself and your loved ones. Or maybe that you need to cut back on the daily Starbucks trips. It also helps you to evaluate whether your current routine is working for you.

When a routine becomes a compulsive need to control, takes away from the enjoyment of life, or causes further stress, it is time to make a change and adjust. This may manifest in feeling overwhelmed or exhausted by doing your routine, bored of the redundancy, or lack of energy and pleasure. On many occasions, I have found myself doing the same routine for months, even though I no longer enjoyed it. Routines are meant to be a regular thing, but that doesn't mean you can't shake it up. Have fun with your routine, try on different ones, switch up what happens each day, keep yourself interested. It does not matter what it looks like. It matters if it feels good.

At the end of the day, you need to find what works for you. It can change week-by-week, month-by-month, change depending on the season of life you're in, change as little or as much as you want. All that must remain the same is consistency and the "why" behind it. A "why" could be to make yourself ready and energized for the day, or it could be to help your mental health. A "why" can sound like "because I want to be as productive as possible but still save time to have fun." It could also sound like "I want to improve my spiritual connection." Your routine should be based on helping you achieve your goals, whether they be physical, emotional, professional, spiritual, social, intellectual, mental, whatever type! If you have a why behind your reason for walking every morning, opening the blinds, reading before bed, exercising every day, going to yoga three times a week, whatever it may be, it will make the routine more pleasurable and more likely to be completed. It does not matter how small the act is or how long it takes. It just needs to work for you. Routines can be incredibly beneficial when done regularly and for the right reason.

You cannot control what happens in life, we know this, but we also know and have learned there are things we *can* control. We can control our thoughts, we can control our reactions, we can control the stories we tell ourselves, and we can control parts of our day via our routines. You can create a routine (morning, midday, night) that is predictable, enjoyable, and allows you to win a part of your day. You can set yourself up for a solid productive day by establishing an energizing and grounding morning routine. You can set yourself up for a restful night's sleep with a relaxing wind-down routine.

ESTABLISHING A SOLID ROUTINE:

1. **Start by figuring out what you want in your routine and what needs to get done.** Ask yourself the following:

   - How do I want to start my day?

   - What do I want to get done in the day?

   - What do I need to get done in a day?

   - What do I want to do less of each day? Things like less screen time, less negative self-talk, and less unhealthy habits.

   - How do I want to end the day?

2. **Make a rough schedule**

   - Once you know the different tasks and activities you want to implement in your daily routine, create a rough schedule so you can fit it all in. Think about when you work best and have the most energy. Think of which tasks might go together and what schedule you already need to follow (i.e., when your classes are). If it helps, break your routine up into a morning, midday, and night routine. You can add time blocks if that works for you, but it is not necessary. Life will always get in the way of even the most structured and detailed routines, so always allow for flexibility.

3. **Try out different routines and experiment to find what feels good**. Routines are completely personal, so test out a few different routines to find the best one for you. Test drive a routine for a few days or weeks before deciding if it is or is not for you.

- Try working out in the morning for a few days and then working out at night for a few days. See which one you enjoy more.
- Experiment with reading before bed or watching television before bed. Does reading help you relax and sleep well, or does relaxing in front of the television work better?
- Does having an ultra-productive Monday through Wednesday and a less hectic Thursday and Friday make you feel less stressed, or would you rather spread work throughout the week?
- Keep making tweaks until you find your sweet spot.

At the end of the day, we all know life is short. I often need to be reminded of this in order to get out of my own head and truly relish in the present moment. Life is *so* short. So, spend the time doing things you like to do! That brings you feelings of joy and presence. Establish a routine that works for you and allows you to tackle and live each day to the fullest.

Routines are a special tool. Use them to your advantage.

CHAPTER 18

ONE PERCENT AT A TIME

———

"Every action you take is a vote for the person you wish to become."

—JAMES CLEAR; AUTHOR

When I started training for my half marathon, running seemed unnatural and took a lot of motivation and mental energy. Every day it took a certain pattern of events to get me up and out the door. After a while, it started taking me less energy and thought, and by two months, my prerun routine became habitual.

As you know, I hate running, so the fact I could develop a habit for running bodes well for any habit you wish to adopt.

Let's start by getting clear on what a habit is and its formation.

Habits are behaviors repeated regularly and, after a certain amount of time, performed subconsciously. Habits are generally formed in a three-step pattern: reminder, routine, reward (Harvard Health, 2016). A reminder is any trigger that initiates the behavior—for example, seeing your toothbrush on your bathroom sink or your coffee pot on the counter. Routine is the behavior or action. It is the habit itself, such as brushing your teeth or brewing your coffee. A reward is a benefit we get from the action. The benefit of brushing your teeth is a minty fresh breath, and the benefit of making coffee is a hot cup of coffee and feeling more awake.

BREAKING BAD HABITS

We can use this three-step pattern—the three R's—to help us make or break behaviors. Breaking a bad habit starts with identifying and understanding what the reminder and routine are. Let's say you have developed a bad habit of scrolling for hours on social media before bed. The first step is to understand and shine a light on what activities lead to the routine, what your triggers are. Research has found that the typical habit triggers fall into five categories: time, location, emotional state, preceding event, and other people (Harvard Health, 2016). Using the bad habit of excess phone time, the triggers may look something like:

Time: bedtime

Location: bedroom

Emotional state: tired and lonely

Preceding event: getting into bed, lights off, and phone on the bed

Other people: none

Once we know our triggers, we can begin to disrupt the chain of events by adding in new cues or changing old ones. In this case, we could charge the phone on the other side of the room so it is not next to the bed and rather than going on our phone, leave a book or journal on the bed to prompt us to do that instead.

It is important to ask ourselves why we do the things we do. To identify the cues and circumstances that lead to the habits. When we gain introspection into our behaviors and emotions, we are better equipped to work on changing our habits from the source. It could be that you realize loneliness is to blame for being on your phone at night. Knowing this, you might instead shift to creating a habit of calling a friend before bed or having tea with a roommate.

ADDING GOOD HABITS

If we want to start implementing a new habit into our routine, we can use something to trigger that behavior. Let's say you wanted to start a habit of working out every morning. Every night you could lay out your gym clothes, pack your gym bag, and place it by the door. In the morning, when your alarm wakes you up, you see the gym clothes and bag already set up. Although you may be tempted to snooze and go back to bed, the gym gear acts as a reminder of the habit you want to create. You are more likely to get up and follow through if a cue is set up for you.

When forming new habits, we want to be sure that each habit is rewarded. Rewards are an integral part of the habit pattern; when we have positive reinforcement, we are more motivated to keep performing the action. Some behaviors come with rewards; the reward of working out is endorphins, higher energy, better mood, lower risk of disease, increased strength, and endurance. Some behaviors may require rewards or additional benefits to keep motivating you. Rewards can be anything that is pleasurable for you. Maybe a reward for washing the dishes right away is listening to a podcast you love. Eating healthily all week may result in a meal out at your favorite restaurant. If you work out five times a week for a month, you will buy yourself a new workout set. Whatever the reward is, make sure you are rewarding the habits you want to keep around!

How long do you think a habit takes to form? You might have heard it takes thirty days. In actuality, researchers have found on average, it takes approximately sixty-six days (two months) to make a behavior become automatic, with the range tending to be between eighteen days and two hundred fifty-four days (Clear, 2020). Although these numbers can seem daunting, the more consistent you are, the more likely a habit is to stick and soon, it will become something that you don't have to consciously think about doing. And the more you do it, the easier it becomes.

It might shock you to know that according to researchers at Duke University, habits account for about 40 percent of our behaviors on any given day (Clear, 2014). Forty percent of our day is driven by subconscious behaviors! That's a whole lot of our day!

Even though it can seem hard, painful, boring, and tiring to develop a new habit, before you know it, it will become a part of your daily routine and lifestyle. Forty percent, to be exact.

OUR HABITS SHAPE US

Aristotle, a Greek philosopher who died in 384 BC, once said, "We are what we repeatedly do. Excellence then is not an act, but a habit."

Even in ancient Greece, people already knew the power of habits.

Considering 40 percent of our day is driven by our habits and our habits shape who we are, then the person we are today is a reflection of our past routines and current everyday behaviors. And the person we want to become can be created by building habits to be in line with that identity.

. . .

"We can define who we are by what we do, not the other way around. If you want to be a runner, it helps to run. If you want to be a writer, write... If you wait for perfect, you are hiding."

—Seth Godin

. . .

We can become who we want to be via the habits we create. By thinking, "What does this person's lifestyle look like? What kinds of things does this person do every day?" we are creating our routines and forming new habits based on those behaviors.

OUTCOMES, SYSTEMS, AND IDENTITIES

In his book *Atomic Habits*, James Clear compared change to an onion, saying it occurs on three levels. The outer layer is our outcomes, which are concerned with results. Outcomes are the goals we wish to accomplish, such as losing weight, writing a book, or running a half marathon. The middle layer is our process, the systems we implement to build the habit. A process would look like a workout schedule, an outline and deadlines for writing a book, and developing a training plan for running. The last layer is about changing our identity.

As James Clear wrote, "This level is concerned with changing your beliefs: your worldview, your self-image, your judgments about yourself and others. Most of the beliefs, assumptions, and biases you hold are associated with this level."

Outcomes are the results. Processes are the systems and actions you take. Identity is what you believe.

Many of us just wish to get a result. We start from the outside, the outcomes, and focus on what we want. I have always lived my life this way, using the goal to direct my actions. But the problem with this, with outcome-based habits, is that it just focuses on the results, not the necessary and effective steps to get there. In order to successfully achieve a goal, we need to focus on the systems we put in place.

Goals may direct where we want to go, they are the destination we hope to end up at, but our systems get us there. They are our map or, in today's world, our Google Maps app. To get to our destination (our goal), we need directions to get us there (our systems).

Let's say our goal is to lose weight (our outcome). If we focus solely on this, we may just jump right in, restricting calories, overexercising, partaking in fad diets, and diet industry-laden products. While yes, in the short-term, this may cause us to lose weight, this is an unhealthy, unsustainable weight loss, and we are likely to gain the weight back. When we reach the result, we tend to stop implementing the same systems we did before. We stop going to the gym, eating healthily, hydrating. Often, we just care about getting to the destination, and once we get there, we give up on the systems.

If, instead, we took a systems-based approach to lose weight, we would start by creating a workout plan and moving our bodies more. We would increase our water intake and add in more fruits, vegetables, and lean proteins. We would cut back on sugar and processed foods. We would create healthier habits and focus on shifting our actions to be more in-line with health and well-being. Our focus would be on changing our actions and behaviors. Weight loss would happen, but it is not our main focus. Our main goal is to develop habits that we will sustain for years to come.

Getting to the outcome is a quick fix, check mark, and temporary solution, but we are not developing proper habits. It's like cleaning your room once and then waiting until it gets overly messy to do it again. When we focus on the systems, the actions, and the steps we take, we are able to build long-lasting habits. We start putting our clothes away, making the bed and tidying up every day. We follow the system and always have a clean room.

But perhaps one of the best methods for getting better outcomes is by focusing on identity-based habits, making habits from the inside out.

James Clear coined the term "identity-based habits," which states our current habits reflect our current identity. There is a strong correlation between our identity and our habits. Writing in his book: "If you're looking to make a change, then I say stop worrying about results and start worrying about your identity. Become the type of person who can achieve the things you want to achieve. Build identity-based habits now. The results can come later."

Taking the same weight loss example, using an identity approach, we change our narrative on who we think we are and how we see ourselves. We adopt an identity of a healthy eater, someone who exercises regularly and cares about taking care of their body. When we believe ourselves to be this person, we act in accordance and start developing systems to eat better, exercise more, hydrate well, sleep enough, and fuel properly. We change ourselves from the inside, which affects our habits, lifestyle, and choices. The changes may lead to the desired result (weight loss), but it could just lead to feeling and looking better, even though the scale doesn't say you lost weight. Our newfound identity habits are more sustainable and likely to persist long after achieving the desired outcome.

From personal experience, I have found identity-based habits to be extremely beneficial. In high school, when I wanted to lose weight, all I cared about was achieving the outcome. I developed outcome-based habits, and while I did end up at my goal weight, I also ended up negatively affecting my physical, mental, and emotional well-being. I did not implement good systems. I did not take the time to create a road map for how I would lose the weight. I just did what I thought I needed to. But since then, I have adopted the identity of someone who cares about health, nutrition, and well-being. I eat a balanced diet, work out regularly, hydrate properly, sleep enough, and I listen to my body's needs. Although I may be heavier than I was in high school, I am happier, healthier, and fitter. I created a new identity, and with that, my systems changed, and other positive outcomes followed.

HOW TO MAKE YOUR HABITS STICK:

1. **Set yourself up for success**

   Make it easy to perform a habit by setting yourself up for success. Place your book on your pillow before bed. Meal prep healthy foods for the week. Set limits on your phone apps. Create written or phone reminders. Use the habit triggers (time, location, emotion, people, previous events) to your advantage.

2. Stack your habits

Stacking habits is finding a way to tie a new habit with an already existing habit. Researchers have found this to be an effective way to implement a new behavior into your routine, as your brain is already primed to support your current habit (Clear, 2020). Just like with exercise and building muscles, the more you use your brain for a habit, the stronger the connection becomes.

Habit stacking can look like every time you drink your coffee in the morning (current habit), you take the time to journal (a habit you want to form). Or, while you brush your teeth, you do twenty squats. The point is to pair a current habit with a new habit, and the current habit must precede the new.

3. Consistency

While habits generally take a while to create, the more we do them, the easier they become, and the faster they integrate into our routine. As we have all heard time and time again, "consistency is key." But the key to consistency is starting small. We are much more likely to stick with something if we build up to it. If we want to start working out but have not done so in months, start small with a short workout video, a walk, or a yoga class. Start by moving your body for a short amount of time and gradually work up to longer, more intense workouts. If we go all-in too soon, we can become discouraged and lose motivation.

4. Reward yourself

Incentives, benefits, rewards, positive reinforcement are one-third of the process of developing habits. They are an integral part and, often, the most fun part! Rewards don't need to be big; they don't need to involve money or food. It can be as simple as watching a TV show while you walk on the treadmill or crossing off something on your to-do list.

HABITS TO HELP YOU BE YOU AND TO BE HAPPY:

When thinking of some new habits you may what to implement, I recommend adding in some of the following suggestions. These habits have helped me feel my best and learn more about who I am at my core. They have helped me become more attuned with my body and more self-aware.

1. Meditation

Meditation is huge for many reasons. Meditation helps to improve your memory, mood, immune system function, focus, self-image, sleep, and stress response (Hayes, 2020). The more you do it, the better you will be at connecting to your inner self and tuning out the noise around you and in your own mind. Meditation will help you get closer to your inner guide and hear more wisdom from within. Start with only a few minutes and gradually build. Like anything, it takes practice!

2. Journaling

Journaling is not only incredibly therapeutic, but it also helps you become aware of your subconscious thoughts and feelings. Spend time every day or a few days each week journaling freely. Put pen to paper with no agenda and just write what is on your mind. It is important not to judge yourself for the thoughts you have. Just let your feelings and thoughts be as they are. You are just an observer of them. Who knows what you may discover about yourself through this activity.

3. Exercise

Exercise is as much for mental health and clarity as it is for physical benefits. Exercise for your mind as much as you do it for your body. Do exercises that work for you and you love doing. I hate running, so I don't run. I love spinning, so I spin as many times a week as I want to. I have found that when I exercise just to burn as many calories as I can, I think of the exercise as punishment, feel less motivated, and don't enjoy it. But when I exercise because I care about my body, mental health, and I want more energy, I am more motivated to work out and enjoy it so much more!

4. Nutrition and Hydration

Eat healthy foods to fuel your body and make it run efficiently but also eat yummy foods because everything is about balance, and life is too short to not eat cake. It is also important to stay hydrated throughout the day. Water is essential for our body's functioning. It helps bring nutrients and oxygen to our cells, flush toxins out of our body, aid in proper organ functioning, among many other benefits (McIntosh, 2018). When we are well hydrated, we have more energy, better digestion, and clearer skin.

5. Nature

Spend time outdoors, not on your phone, and connect with nature. Take time every day and step outside, even just for a moment. Fresh air can do wonders.

6. Sleep

Sleep is extremely important. For most young adults, we need seven to nine hours of sleep a night. When we sleep, we are allowing our brain and body to repair, reenergize, and restore. Sleep helps with memory formation, learning, emotional stability, cell repair, and cell growth. This allows us to work and function properly throughout the day. When we don't sleep enough or have poor sleep, we become irritable, make bad decisions, become sick easily, have trouble concentrating, and gain weight (Nunez and Lamoreux, 2020).

7. Gratitude

When we take time to think or write down what we are grateful for, it puts everything in perspective, and the minor inconveniences that bubble up every day don't seem so dramatic. Gratitude re-aligns us with what matters in life and all the blessings we have. Gratitude does not have to be about shiny, fancy things. Even taking a moment to be grateful for sunny weather or a good cup of coffee can bring feelings of joy. Every time I start my day writing down three to five things I am grateful for, I find myself feeling more centered, even-keel, and I end up appreciating my day more.

8. Here and Now

Be here and now. Every day, for as much of the day as you can, live in the moment fully. All we ever have is the current moment. When we live in the moment and don't think of the future or what happened in the past, we live more stress-free and live more grounded. When I live in the moment, I feel more connected to my body and my surroundings. I am more attuned to my body's needs, my swirling thoughts, and my inner knowing.

ONE PERCENT EVERY DAY

In *Atomic Habits,* author James Clear found that "if you can get 1 percent better each day for one year, you'll end up thirty-seven times better by the time you're done. Conversely, if you get 1 percent worse each day for one year, you'll decline nearly down to zero."

"One percent worse every day for one year. $0.99\char`^365 = 00.03$"
"One percent better every day for one year. $1.01\char`^365 = 37.78$"

Doing one thing every day to set yourself up for success, even the most minuscule of things, can have a dramatic positive effect in the long run. The habits we adopt today will change who we are a week, month, and year from now.

What can you do each day to become 1 percent better?

CHAPTER 19

LETTER TO THE READER

Dear Reader,

First, I want to thank you for taking the time to read this book. It means so much to me that you would spend your time and energy on this passion project of mine.

I know in the introduction I wrote my intent on why I wrote this book. That still holds true, but as I am finishing, I also realize I wrote this book because I believe everyone has the potential and the ability to live the life they want and dream of. I wrote this book to hopefully give you some tools that have helped me work toward the life I want to live, a life I will look back on and smile with pride and a full heart.

I wrote this book over my senior year of college during COVID-19. This year challenged us all in many ways, not just with the pandemic, but the stark political divide, the violence, social injustice, and horrendous acts of racism.

I personally struggled deeply with uncertainty, loss, isolation, sadness, and poor self-esteem. It was a hard year, one that has changed me in many ways—a year of some ups but many downs. While I will not look back on the year with fond memories, I will always try and remember the lessons I gained.

I learned to never take anything for granted, to enjoy as much as I can at any moment. I was reminded even on the hard days there is so much to be thankful for—even if it is just the sun shining or a good cup of coffee. I experienced how resilient we are—we can adapt to any situation. I witnessed the power of asking for help when you need it. I understood the power of a story. That when I changed my story, I changed my outlook, my emotions, my actions, and belief of self.

On my low days, my story kept me stuck. On the days I turned the page to a new story, by consciously changing my thoughts to be more positive and in line with who I am, my story changed the game. All I can control is myself.

This book wasn't always easy to write, but my goal throughout was to be honest. I know some stories were deeper or more relatable than others. Some were hard to write, while others made me smile. But all of what I shared was to express that you are never alone. We are all human, dealing with many of the same challenges and insecurities, learning to give ourselves love and compassion, constantly working on bettering ourselves, and moving forward. Things may look different between our journeys and stories, but we all share the same end goal: to be happy, to love, and to be loved.

I encourage you to open up a notebook sometime soon and freely write about how you are feeling, what you love about your life, what you are grateful for, what you want more of, what is lacking, what your life would look like in your dream world. The answers are within you. Find them and start working toward what you want. I know I am.

I hope one day soon you can look in the mirror and feel happy with the person you are and excited about the person you are becoming. I hope that you are able to find happiness and joy in the here and now and know at any point in life, you are never stuck—in a mere moment, things can change, you can change. What you want in life is available to you. Abundance is accessible, and with the right tools, state of mind, and actions, it is yours. I believe in you; I hope you believe in you too.

I also hope you know that you are loved and adored whether you are aware of it or not. Keep those people close and tell them you love them whenever you get the chance. Life is too short to hold back hugs and messages of love.

And above all, I hope you always stay true to yourself, stay true to your dreams. I hope you can be you and be happy.

Love,

Livia

ACKNOWLEDGMENTS

———

First and foremost, I'd like to thank my parents, Stephanie and Vittorio. Without your love, support, and advice, I would not be where I am today, and this book would not have been written. I am beyond grateful to be your daughter, and for all the opportunities you have given me.

A big thank you to my three beta readers: Justin O'Neill, Jennifer O'Neill, and Penny Doud. Thank you for taking time out of your busy schedules to read some of my chapters and provide helpful suggestions and advice. I greatly appreciate it!

A special thank you to all of my first supporters who were excited to read this book and help me make it a reality: Monique Reyes, Grace Bellman, Hannah Fleischmann, Savannah Bulloch, Maria Rojas, Hailey Karten, Alexa Frandzel, Emma Butler, Emma Folkart, Mark Michael, Maggie Prieto, Eric Michael, Craig Kruger, Juli Michael, Judy and Frank Haims, Craig Haims, Jane Armstrong, Wilson Haims, Emma Haims, Stephanie Haims, Vittorio Severino, Massimo Severino, Nina Rossiter, Jennifer O'Neill, Justin O'Neill, Kristen O'Neill, Janet Michael, Felisa Michael, Olivia Michael, Anna Sullivan, Cameron Sullivan, Marcy Michael, Penny Doud, Katherine

Brannack, Radhika Kadakia, Bianca Fantacci, Edoardo Fantacci, Roma Bartel, Talin Megherian, Sarah Lundal, Jeanne Hamilton, Daria Zarzeka, Kate Allan, Sasha Dymant, Natalie Henning, Fiona Bertic, Lieve Lichter, Savanna Clegg, Carolina Ramos, Neha Gundavarapu, Ankita John, Ruiy Shah, Rob Hoffman, Sue Applebaum, David Jackins, Dana Sinno, Cammie Lesser, Laura Kara, Casey Aitken, and Eric Koester. All of your support means so much!

Thank you to my interviewees, Katy Bellotte and Brooke Miccio. I appreciate you taking the time to talk with me about your passions, life, and careers. You are both doing incredible things.

I would also like to give a *huge* thank you to the New Degree Press team, especially Eric Koester, Brian Bies, Amanda Munro, and Faiqa Zafar, for helping me every step of the way and making the whole process enjoyable.

If you have played a role in my life at any point, thank you for the memories, experiences, learning lessons, or good stories. Whether we still talk to this day or haven't in years, I will forever cherish the time we had.

Lastly, thank you to my readers for taking a chance on me and reading this book. Even though I may not know you, I am here for you.

APPENDIX

CHAPTER 1: LEAN INTO BODY LOVE

Muhlheim, Lauren. "The Connection Between Body Image and Eating Disorders." *Verywell Mind,* January 15, 2021. www.verywellmind.com/body-image-and-eating-disorders-4149424#citation-1.

National Association of Anorexia Nervosa and Associated Disorders. "Eating Disorder Statistics: General & Diversity Stats." Accessed June 23, 2021. https://anad.org/get-informed/about-eating-disorders/eating-disorders-statistics/

National Eating Disorders Association. "Body Image & Eating Disorders." February 22, 2018. https://www.nationaleatingdisorders.org/body-image-eating-disorders.

US Department of Health and Human Services. "Rate of Eating Disorders in Kids Keeps Rising." July 18, 2011. http://www.healthfinder.gov/news/newsstory.aspx?docID=646574

CHAPTER 2: INSECURITIES AND VULNERABILITIES

Hilliard, Jena. "Social Media Addiction." *Addiction Center,* March 30, 2021. https://www.addictioncenter.com/drugs/social-media-addiction/.

McDavid, Jodi. *The Social Dilemma*. Journal of Religion & Film: Vol. 24: Iss. 1, Article 22. 2020, Netflix, 94 min.

Nordqvist, Christian. "Eating Disorders Among Fashion Models Rising." *Medical News Today*, July 8, 2007. https://www.medicalnewstoday.com/articles/76241#1.

Runfola, Cristin D, et al., "Body dissatisfaction in women across the lifespan: results of the UNC-SELF and Gender and Body Image (GABI) studies." *European eating disorders review: the journal of the Eating Disorders Association* 21, no.1 (January 2013): 52–9. https://doi:10.1002/erv.2201

Yotka, Steff. "How Sara Ziff and more than 40 other models are leading the charge against eating disorders." Vogue, February 1, 2017. https://www.vogue.com/article/model-alliance-eating-disorder-study.

CHAPTER 3: FACETUNE, FOMO, AND THE COMPARISON TRAP

Cherry, Kendra. "Social Comparison Theory in Psychology." *Verywell Mind*, September 20, 2020. https://www.verywellmind.com/what-is-the-social-comparison-process-2795872.

Hunt, Melissa G., et al. "No More FOMO: Limiting Social Media Decreases Loneliness and Depression." *Journal of Social and Clinical Psychology* 37, no. 10 (December 2018): 751–768. https://doi:10.1521/jscp.2018.37.10.751.

Murray, Rheana. "Social Media Is Affecting the Way We View Our Bodies—and It's Not Good." *TODAY*, May 8, 2018. https://www.today.com/style/social-media-affecting-way-we-view-our-bodies-it-s-t128500. Tiggemann, Marika, and Amy Slater. "NetTweens: The Internet and Body Image Concerns in Preteenage Girls." *The Journal of Early Adolescence* 34, no. 5 (September 2013): 606–620. https://doi:10.1177/0272431613501083.

CHAPTER 4: HAPPINESS GOES WHERE HAPPINESS IS

Brickman, Philip, Dan Coates, and Ronnie Janoff-Bulman. "Lottery winners and accident victims: Is happiness relative?" *Journal of Personality and Social Psychology* 36, no. 8, (1978): 917–927. https://doi.org/10.1037/0022-3514.36.8.917

Gilbert, Daniel. "The Surprising Science of Happiness." Filmed February 2004. TED video, 20.52. https://www.ted.com/talks/dan_gilbert_the_surprising_science_of_happiness

Goldhill, Olivia. "Neuroscience Confirms That to Be Truly Happy, You Will Always Need Something More." *Quartz*, May 15, 2016. https://www.qz.com/684940/neuroscience-confirms-that-to-be-truly-happy-you-will-always-need-something-more/.

Jackson, Sarah E., et al. "Psychological Changes Following Weight Loss in Overweight and Obese Adults: A Prospective Cohort Study." *PLoS ONE* 9, no. 8 (August 2014): https://doi:10.1371/journal.pone.0104552.

Kahneman, Daniel, and Angus Deaton. "High Income Improves Evaluation of Life but Not Emotional Well-Being." *Proceedings of the National Academy of Sciences* 107, no. 38 (September 2010): 16489–16493. https://doi:10.1073/pnas.1011492107.

Levine, Linda J., et al., "Accuracy and Artifact: Reexamining the Intensity Bias in Affective Forecasting." *Journal of Personality and Social Psychology,* no. 4 (August 2012): 584–605. https://doi:10.1037/a0030370.

Lyubomirsky, Sonja, Kennon. M. Sheldon, and David Schkade. "Pursuing Happiness: The Architecture of Sustainable Change." *Review of General Psychology,* no. 2 (June 2005): 111–131. https://doi:10.1037/1089-2680.9.2.111

Myers, David. G. *The American Paradox: Spiritual Hunger in an Age of Plenty.* Yale University Press, 2000.

Weinschenk, Susan. "The Dopamine Seeking-Reward Loop." *Psychology Today,* February 28, 2018. https://www.psychologytoday.com/us/blog/brain-wise/201802/the-dopamine-seeking-reward-loop#:~:text=But%20then%20research%20began%20to,fuels%20your%20searching%20for%20information.

CHAPTER 5: YOU ARE YOUR MOST IMPORTANT RELATIONSHIP

Brown, Brené. *Gifts of Imperfection: Let Go of Who You Think You're Supposed to Be and Embrace Who You Are.* Hazelden Publishing, 2010.

Robbins, Mel. "How To Stop Screwing Yourself." Filmed June 2011 in San Fransisco, CA. TED video, 21:39. https://www.ted.com/talks/mel_robbins_how_to_stop_screwing_yourself_over?language=en

Shapiro, Hannah. "Dove's Campaign for Real Beauty boosts girls' self-esteem for Back to School." *Examiner.com,* March 3, 2014. http://www.examiner.com/article/dove-s-campaign-for-real-beauty-boosts-girls-self-esteem-for-back-to-school.

CHAPTER 6: BE THE MAIN CHARACTER IN YOUR LIFE

Ashley Graham. "Elaine Welteroth on Trailblazing and Making The Jump | Pretty Big Deal." March 10, 2020. Video, 51:01. https://www.youtube.com/watch?v=HIY8A8ccfKM

Breakfast Club Power 105.1 FM. "Elaine Welteroth Describes Why You Are 'More Than Enough', Her Journey From Intern To Editor + More." June 11, 2019. Video, 28:53. https://www.youtube.com/watch?v=ibiKup47nec

Steiner, Susie. "Top Five Regrets of the Dying." *The Guardian*, February 1, 2012. www.theguardian.com/lifeandstyle/2012/feb/01/top-five-regrets-of-the-dying.

Ware, Bronnie. *The Top Five Regrets of the Dying: A Life Transformed by the Dearly Departing.* Hay House Inc., 2012.

Welteroth, Elaine. *More Than Enough: Claiming Space for Who You Are.* New York: Penguin Random House, 2019.

CHAPTER 7: THANK YOU... NEXT ONE!

Carter, Sherrie Bourg. "The Hidden Health Hazards of Toxic Relationships." *Psychology Today,* August 7, 2011. https://www.psychologytoday.com/us/blog/high-octane-women/201108/the-hidden-health-hazards-toxic-relationships.

Edwards, Katie. M., Christine A. Gidycz, and Megan J Murphy. "College women's stay/leave decisions in abusive dating relationships: A prospective analysis of an expanded investment model." *Journal of Interpersonal Violence* 26, no.7 (June 2010): 1446–1462. https://doi.org/10.1177/0886260510369131

Fletcher, G. O., J. A. Simpson, and G. Thomas. "Ideals, perceptions, and evaluations in early relationship development." *Journal of Personality and Social Psychology* 79, no. 6 (December 2000): 933–940. https://doi: 10.1037//0022-3514.79.6.933.

Forbes."Research Shows Bad Relationships Can Also Mean Bad Health." May 3, 2018. https://www.forbes.com/sites/quora/2018/05/03/research-shows-bad-relationships-can-also-mean-bad-health/?sh=286b29191d5e.

Fugère, Madeleine A. "6 Reasons Why We Stay in Bad Relationships." *Psychology Today,* May 4, 2017. https://www.

psychologytoday.com/us/blog/dating-and-mating/201705/6-reasons-why-we-stay-in-bad-relationships.

Luciano, E. C., and U. Orth. "Transitions in romantic relationships and development of self-esteem." *Journal of Personality and Social Psychology* 112, no.2 (February 2017): 307–328. https://doi:10.1037/pspp0000109

Rego, Sara, Joana Arantes, and Paula Magalhães. "Is there a Sunk Cost Effect in Committed Relationships?" *Current Psychology* 37, no. 12 (September 2018): 1–12. https://doi:10.1007/s12144-016-9529-9

Villines, Zawn. "Red Flags: Are You Being Emotionally Manipulated?" *GoodTherapy*, September 20, 2019. https://www.goodtherapy.org/blog/red-flags-are-you-being-emotionally-manipulated-0917197.

CHAPTER 8: GO ALL-IN

Bokhari, Dean. "Action Leads to Motivation (Not the Other Way around)." *Dean Bokhari—Self Improvement Classes*, September 9, 2020. https://www.deanbokhari.com/acton-leads motivation/#:~:text=Regardless%20of%20what%20you%20want,is%20the%20precursor%20to%20motivation

Corporate Finance Institute. "SMART Goal—Definition, Guide, and Importance of Goal Setting." September 16, 2020. https://www.corporatefinanceinstitute.com/resources/knowledge/other/smart-goal/#:~:text=A%20SMART%20goal%20is%20used,chances%20of%20achieving%20your%20goal.

McRaven, William H. "Adm. McRaven Urges Graduates to Find Courage to Change the World." *UT News*, May 16, 2014. https://www.news.utexas.edu/2014/05/16/mcraven-urges-graduates-to-find-courage-to-change-the-world/.

Mel Robbins. "The 5 Second Rule." December 13, 2018. https://www.melrobbins.com/the-5-second-rule/.

Tabaka, Marla. "New Study Says This Simple Step Will Increase the Odds of Achieving Your Goals (Substantially)." *Inc.*, January 28, 2019. https://www.inc.com/marla-tabaka/this-study-found-1-simple-step-to-practically-guarantee-youll-achieve-your-goals-for-real.html.

CHAPTER 9: IT'S OKAY NOT TO BE OKAY

"Oprah Winfrey." February 17, 2021. https://www.biography.com/media-figure/oprah-winfrey.

Feloni, Richard. "Tony Robbins Started out as a Broke Janitor—Then He Saved a Week's Worth of Pay, and the Way He Spent It Changed His Life." *Business Insider*, October 4, 2017. https://

www.businessinsider.com/tony-robbins-changed-his-life-at-17-years-old-2017-10.

Health for a Better World. "Help Your Neighbors and Your Heart: Being Kind Has Many Health Benefits." February 13, 2021. https://www.providence.org/news/uf/645902917.

Taylor, Jill Bolte. *My Stroke of Insight: a Brain Scientist's Personal Journey*. New York: Viking, 2008.

US Library of Congress. Congressional Research Service. *Unemployment Rates During the COVID-19 Pandemic: In Brief*, by Gene Falk et al. R46554. 2021.

CHAPTER 10: PASSIONS ARE PRIORITIES

Cherry, Kendra. "How to Achieve Flow." *Verywell Mind*, April 9, 2021. https://www.verywellmind.com/what-is-flow-2794768.

Ed Mylett. "HOW TO START with Marie Forleo." December 17, 2019. Video, 41.11. https://www.youtube.com/watch?v=aI7zsuZdwUw

McRaven, William H. "Adm. McRaven Urges Graduates to Find Courage to Change the World." *UT News*, May 16, 2014. https://www.news.utexas.edu/2014/05/16/mcraven-urges-graduates-to-find-courage-to-change-the-world/.

Music Ally. "Podcast Listening on Spotify Grew by 175% in 2018." January 19, 2019. https://www.musically.com/2019/01/18/podcast-listening-on-spotify-grew-by-175-in-2018/.

Schumer, Lizz. "Why Following Your Passions Is Good for You (and How to Get Started)." *The New York Times,* October 11, 2018. https://www.nytimes.com/2018/10/10/smarter-living/follow-your-passion-hobbies-jobs-self-care.html.

CHAPTER 11: LIVING LIFE ON YOUR TERMS

Cherry, Kendra. "What Causes Learned Helplessness?" *Verywell Mind*, April 5, 2021. https://www.verywellmind.com/what-is-learned-helplessness-2795326.

Psychology Today. "Learned Helplessness." Accessed May 10, 2021. https://www.psychologytoday.com/us/basics/learned-helplessness.

CHAPTER 12: MOVING THROUGH FEAR

Saad, Nardine. "Oprah Winfrey Says She Faced Fear of Balloons, Made It a Metaphor." *Los Angeles Times*, September 10, 2013. https://www.latimes.com/entertainment/gossip/la-et-mg-oprah-winfrey-afraid-of-balloons-20130910-story.html.

CHAPTER 13: LABELS, THOUGHTS, BELIEFS, OH MY!

Einstein, Gabrielle. "Emotional Guidance Scale by Abraham-Hicks: How to Use It." *Gabby Bernstein*, February 24, 2020. https://www.gabbybernstein.com/emotional-guidance-scale-abraham-hicks/.

Byrne, Rhonda. *The Secret*. Syndey: Atria Books and Beyond Works Publishing, 2006

Cherry, Kendra. "Why Our Brains Are Hardwired to Focus on the Negative." *Verywell Mind*, April 29, 2020. https://www.verywellmind.com/negative-bias-4589618

Comaford, Christine. "Got Inner Peace? 5 Ways To Get It NOW." *Forbes*, November 7, 2013. https://www.forbes.com/sites/christinecomaford/2012/04/04/got-inner-peace-5-ways-to-get-it-now/?sh=3056252c6672.

Hurst, Katherine. "The Power of Thought: Reality Check, Everything Is Energy!" *The Law Of Attraction*, April 16, 2019. https://www.thelawofattraction.com/the-power-of-thoughts/.

Raghunathan, Raj. "How Negative Is Your 'Mental Chatter'?" *Psychology Today*, October 10, 2013. https://www.psychologytoday.com/us/blog/sapient-nature/201310/how-negative-is-your-mental-chatter.

Scott, Elizabeth. "Let the Law of Attraction Help You With Positive Change." *Verywell Mind*, November 18, 2020. https://www.verywellmind.com/understanding-and-using-the-law-of-attraction-3144808.

Sessums, Christina. "Balance Your Body: Vibrations and Frequencies." *Purely Simple Organic Living*, August 18, 2020. https://www.purelysimpleorganicliving.com/vibrations-frequencies/#:~:text=Vibrations%20refer%20to%20the%20oscillating,and%20particles%20caused%20 by%20energy.&text=Frequency%2C%20which%20is%20 measured%20in,determine%20and%20differentiate%20 vibrational%20patterns.

Stanborough, Rebecca Joy. "What Is Vibrational Energy? Definition, Benefits & More." *Healthline*, November 13, 2020. https://www.healthline.com/health/vibrational-energy#:~:text=Vibrational%20energy%20experts%20 claim%20that,evidence%20to%20support%20this%20 correlation.

CHAPTER 14: UNLOCKING THE POWER OF YOUR MIND

Cherry, Kendra. "How Does the Placebo Effect Work?" *Verywell Mind*, April 25, 2021. https://www.verywellmind.com/what-is-the-placebo-effect-2795466.

Crum, Alia. "Change Your Mindset, Change the Game." Filmed in October 2014, in Traverse City. TEDx video, 18:20. https://www.youtube.com/watch?v=0tqq66zwa7g

Hunter, Andy. "It's All In Your Mind? What the Placebo Effect Tells Us." *Brain World*, May 16, 2019. https://www.brainworldmagazine.com/its-all-in-your-mind-what-the-placebo-effect-tells-us/.

CHAPTER 15: YOUR INTUITION HAS YOUR BACK

Doyle, Glennon. Untamed. New York: The Dial Press, 2020

Isaacson, Walter. "The Genius of Jobs." *The New York Times*, October 29, 2011. https://www.nytimes.com/2011/10/30/opinion/sunday/steve-jobss-genius.html.

Locke, Connson Chou. "When It's Safe to Rely on Intuition (and When It's Not)." *Harvard Business Review*, February 12, 2020. https://www.hbr.org/2015/04/when-its-safe-to-rely-on-intuition-and-when-its-not.

Lufityanto, Galang, Chris Donkin, and Joel Pearson. "Measuring Intuition: Nonconscious Emotional Information Boosts Decision Accuracy and Confidence." *Psychological Science* 27, no. 5 (April 2016): 622-34. https://doi: 10.1177/0956797616629403

Nierenberg, Cari. "The Science of Intuition: How to Measure 'Hunches' and 'Gut Feelings.'" *LiveScience*, May 20, 2016. https://www.livescience.com/54825-scientists-measure-intuition.html#:~:text=Intuition%20can%20help%20people%20make,their%20conscious%20mind%2C%20he%20said.

Psychology Today. "Intuition." Accessed May 5, 2021. https://www.psychologytoday.com/us/basics/intuition.

CHAPTER 16: LEAVE WHAT DOESN'T SERVE YOU

Brown, Brené. *Gifts of Imperfection: Let Go of Who You Think You're Supposed to Be and Embrace Who You Are.* Hazelden Publishing, 2010.

Sherer Murray, Jill. "The Unstoppable Power of Letting Go." Filmed December 2016, in Wilmington, NC. TEDx video, 11:33. https://www.youtube.com/watch?v=nirKw3mWB3I

CHAPTER 17: THE POWER OF RITUALS

Adams, Bryan. "6 Morning the power of rituals of Steve Jobs, Tony Robbins, Oprah, and Other Successful Leaders." *Inc*, September 7, 2017. https://www.inc.com/bryan-adams/6-celebrity-morning-rituals-to-help-you-kick-ass.html.

Cherry, Kendra. "The Importance of Maintaining Structure and Routine During Stressful Times." *Verywell Mind*, April 21, 2020. https://www.verywellmind.com/the-importance-of-keeping-a-routine-during-stressful-times-4802638.

Forshee, Danielle. "Psychological Benefits of Routines." *Danielle Forshee,* July 2, 2019. https://www.drdanielleforshee.com/psychological-benefits-of-routines/.

Huffington, Arianna. "Arianna Huffington's Morning Routine." *My Morning Routine,* March 21, 2021. https://www.mymorningroutine.com/arianna-huffington/.

Peters, Brandon. "Rise and Shine! Sleep Better and Wake Up at the Same Time Every Day." *Verywell Health,* April 13, 2020. https://www.verywellhealth.com/30-days-to-better-sleep-3973920.

Roomer, Jari. "12 Morning Routine Habits From Highly Successful People." *Medium,* September 2, 2019. https://www.medium.com/personal-growth-lab/12-morning-routine-habits-from-highly-successful-people-c6c56e4e0473.

CHAPTER 18: ONE PERCENT AT A TIME

Clear, James. *Atomic Habits: An Easy & Proven Way to Build Good Habits & Break Bad Ones.* New York: Penguin Random House, 2018.

Clear, James. "Habit Stacking: How to Build New Habits by Taking Advantage of Old Ones." *James Clear,* February 4, 2020. https://www.jamesclear.com/habit-stacking.

Clear, James. "How Long Does It Take to Form a Habit? Backed by Science." *James Clear,* February 4, 2020. https://www.jamesclear.com/new-habit.

Clear, James. "5 Steps to Building a New Habit." *Entrepreneur,* July 30, 2014. https://www.entrepreneur.com/article/235935#:~:text=According%20to%20researchers%20at%20Duke,and%20your%20life%20in%20general.

Harvard Health. *"How Much Water Should You Drink?"* March 25, 2020. https://www.health.harvard.edu/staying-healthy/how-much-water-should-you-drink.

Harvard Health. "Trade Bad Habits for Good Ones." November 9, 2016. https://www.health.harvard.edu/staying-healthy/trade-bad-habits-for-good-ones.

Hayes, Annie. "13 Proven Benefits of Meditation." *Netdoctor,* July 31, 2020. https://www.netdoctor.co.uk/healthy-living/mental-health/a33441611/benefits-meditation/.

McIntosh, James. "15 Benefits of Drinking Water and Other Water Facts." *Medical News Today,* July 16, 2018. https://www.medicalnewstoday.com/articles/290814#benefits.

Nunez, Kirsten and Karen Lamoreux. "Why Do We Sleep?" *Healthline,* July 20, 2020. https://www.healthline.com/health/why-do-we-sleep#amount-of-sleep.